ALI BANISADR. Beautiful Lies

Museo Stefano Bardini,
Florence, April 30 – October 4, 2021

Museo di Palazzo Vecchio, Sala dei Gigli,
Florence, April 30 – September 6, 2021

curated by Sergio Risaliti

ALI BANISADR

Beautiful Lies

FORMA

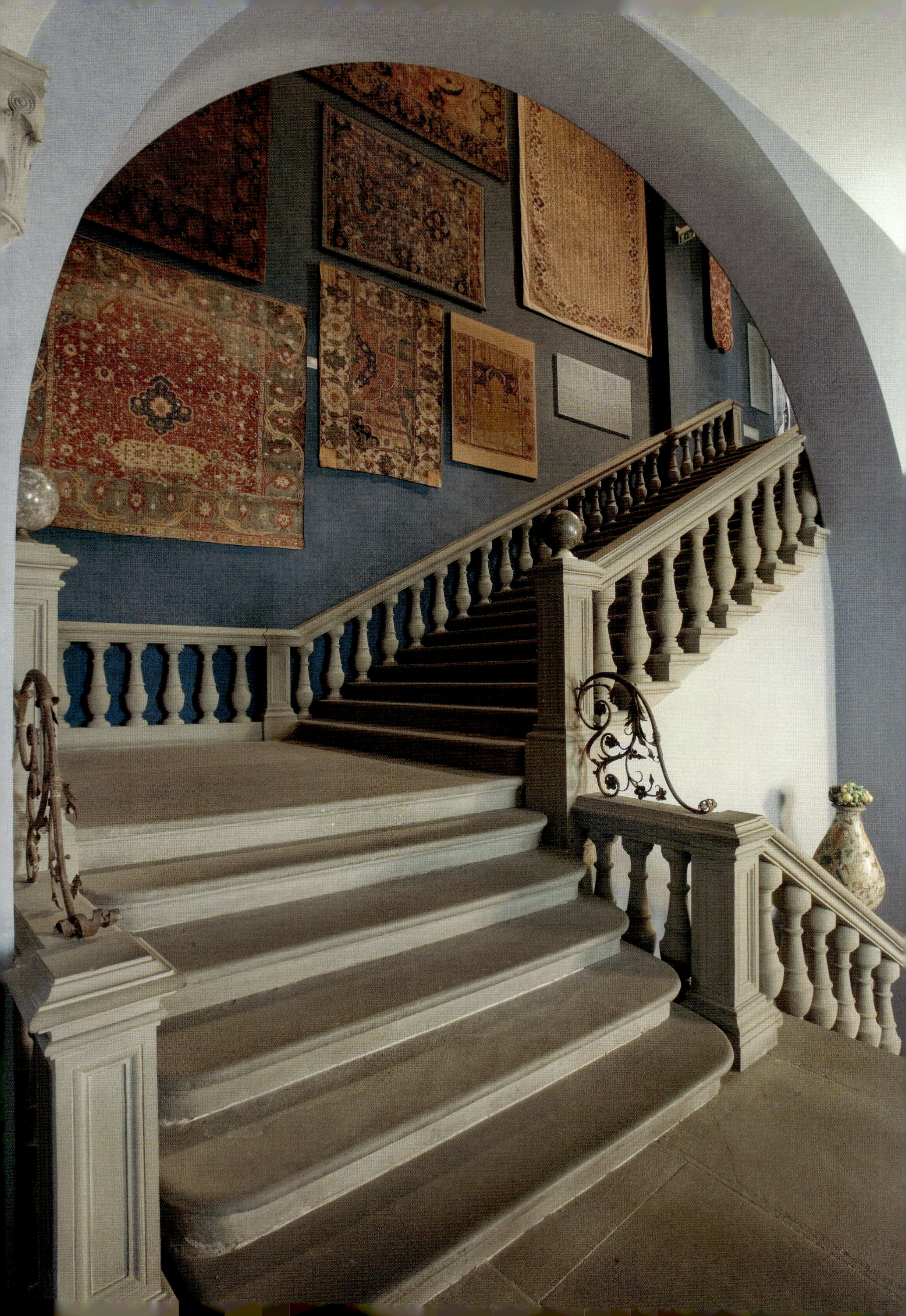

Editor of the catalogue
Sergio Risaliti

Editorial project and production
Forma Edizioni srl, Florence, Italy
redazione@formaedizioni.it
www.formaedizioni.it

Editorial direction
Laura Andreini

Editorial staff
Maria Giulia Caliri
Livia D'Aliasi
Raffaele Moretti
Elena Varani

Graphic design
Valeria Pugliese
Mauro Sampaolesi

Photolithography
Forma Edizioni

Printing
Lito Terrazzi
Prato, Italy

Editorial supervision
for Museo Novecento
Lisa Masolini

Translations
NTL – Il Nuovo
Traduttore Letterario S.c.

Photo credits
Set-up photos © Sergio Dominigie
Artworks photos © Charles Duprat,
Adam Reich, Jeffrey Sturges given by
Galerie Thaddaeus Ropac,
London · Paris · Salzburg

ALI BANISADR. Beautiful Lies
Museo Stefano Bardini,
Florence, April 30 – October 4, 2021
Museo di Palazzo Vecchio,
Sala dei Gigli,
Florence, April 30 – September 6, 2021

Promoted by
Comune di Firenze

Curated by
Sergio Risaliti

Scientific coordination
Francesca Neri – MUS.E

Organization
Luca Puri

Education department
MUS.E

Communication
MUS.E
Costanza Savelloni

Press office
Elisa Di Lupo, Comune di Firenze
Lea Codognato, Caterina Briganti,
Davis & Co.

Graphic design
Dania Menafra

Condition report
Silvia Fiaschi

Art work insurance
UNIQA

Art handling and art work installation
Apice Firenze S.r.l.

Freestanding walls set up
Opera Laboratori Fiorentini S.p.a.

Lights set up
Vannetti Andrea S.r.l.

Graphic prints on display
Fotolito La Progressiva S.r.l.

Surveillance
REAR Società Cooperativa

Thanks to:
Dario Nardella
Mayor of Florence
Tommaso Sacchi
Councillor for Culture, Fashion,
Design and International Relations
of the City of Florence
Matteo Spanò
President of MUS.E

Pietro Alongi, Barbara Basso,
Andrea Batistini, Andrea Bianchi,
Maria Luisa Caccuri, Valentina
Caramante, Mariella Carlotti,
Elena Chiti, Rita Corsini,
Emanuele Crocetti, Gabriella Farsi,
Eva Francioli, Roberto Gabucci,
Daniela Giachi, Susanna Giovannuzzi,
Antonella Nesi, Antonella Nicola,
Silvia Penna, Serena Pini,
Stefania Rispoli, Paolo Sani,
Carmela Valdevies, Lorenzo Valloriani

And all those who have contributed
to the making of this project

The exhibition was realized
in collaboration with:
Thaddaeus Ropac,
London · Paris · Salzburg

First edition: July 2022
ISBN: 978-88-55210-95-9

Page 5:
Museo Stefano Bardini
Interior

Pages 8-9:
Melencolia I
Museo Stefano Bardini

CONTENTS

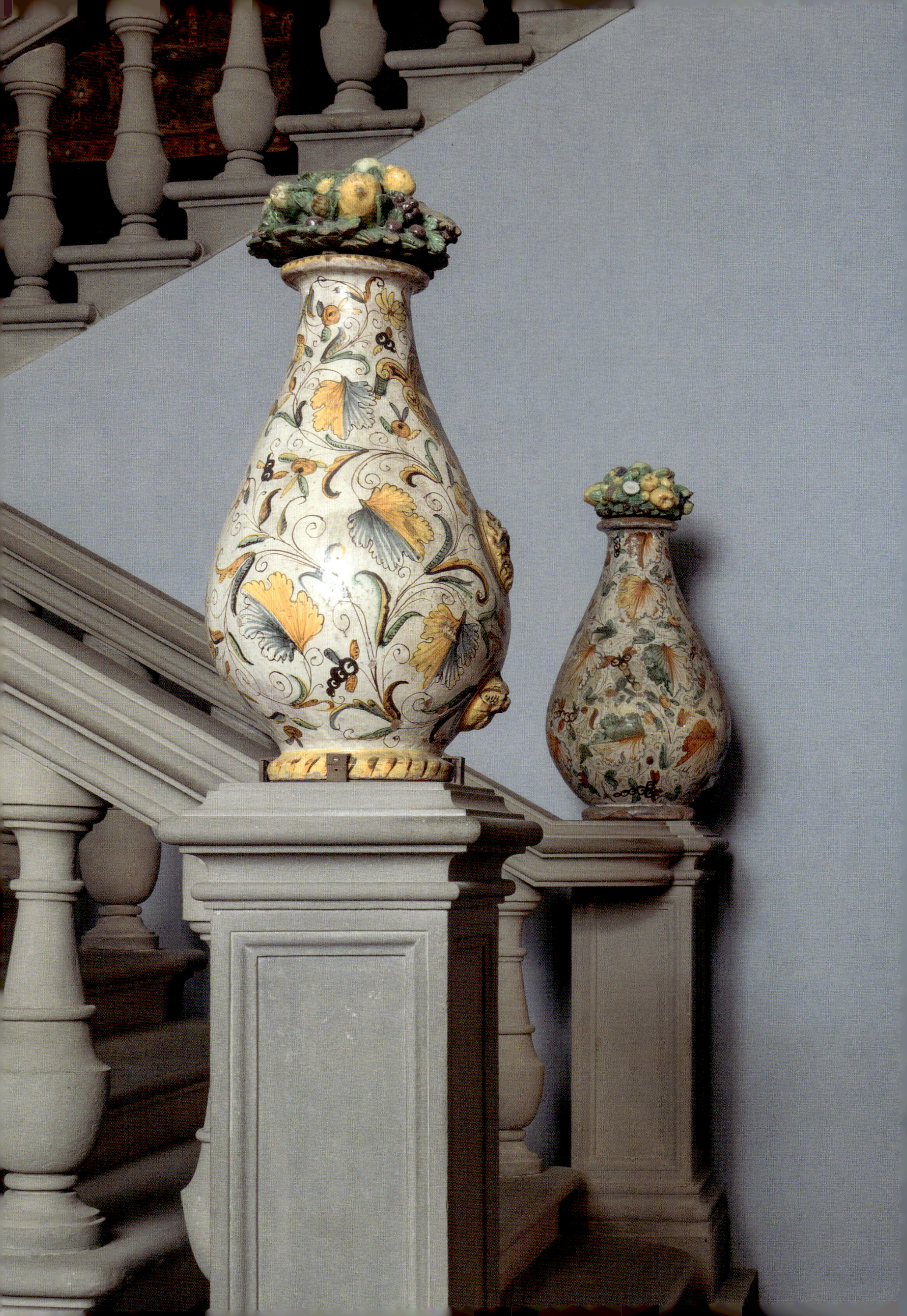

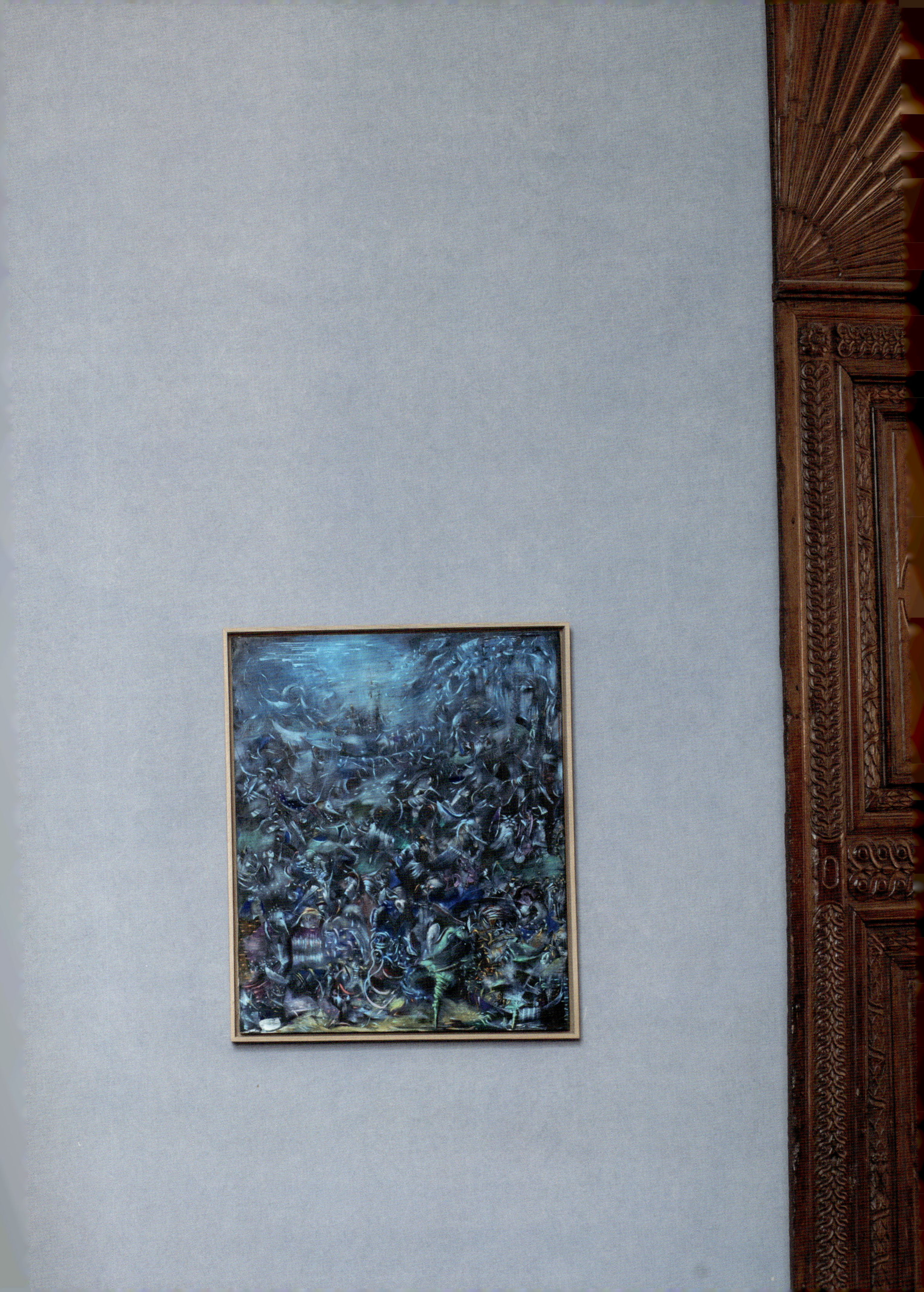

BETWEEN THE PERSONAL AND THE UNIVERSAL: THE PICTURE AS A VAST CONTAINER OF IMAGES AND SENSATIONS

Sergio Risaliti

The tension between modernism and tradition remains unresolved, as does the opposition between surface and plane, easel painting and dripping. Increasingly evident, on the other hand, is the search on the part of contemporary artists, for formal precedents in the art of the past. Specific and individual genealogies, as well as evermore open and diachronic content, encompassing narratives and archetypes, are sought in response to a need for meaning. Contemporary society too seems to demand meaning from an art that is anxious to avoid enclosing itself within its own speculative confines or giving free rein to a mannerism more and more detached from any gnoseological engagement. In a globalized world where cultural borders are increasingly open, and exchanges between artists have proliferated partly due to the extension of the art system, new borders and new paths have become accessible thanks to artists who have found a way to resolve tensions between past and present, between personal memory and universal history, knitting together the tear between modernity and classicism.

When I met Ali Banisadr, I discovered a very knowledgeable artist, not just in the field of art history but music and literature too. His works cannot be separated from his life story, which is marked by dramatic events that have remained impressed upon his memory and, I would say, his body. From poetry he retains archetypes and visions encapsulating the earth and the cosmos; from sound he takes rhythms and chromatic harmonies; from the disasters of war he draws his highly fantastic and surreal visions. Speaking with him about Florence and Dante, I learnt about his great passion for the *Divine Comedy*. So, three years ago, I invited him to make new works for the 700th anniversary of Dante's death, so as to enrich his copious output with a reference that is familiar to us in Florence.

Born in Teheran, Ali Banisadr moved to the United States with his parents when he was still a child. He produced his first drawings in the basement of his home, as everything collapsed around him during bombardments. When he was twenty, he went to San Francisco and discovered the Mission School art scene; he then moved to New York in 2000, where he studied at the School of Visual Arts. In 2006 he won a scholarship to visit Normandy. While exploring the D-Day beaches, Banisadr experienced a kind of 'hallucination': he describes having had the certainty of being in the midst of those past events, reliving the landing physically and "being able to hear the whistling and banging, feeling everything within my body as if it were real and familiar".

That experience was a genuine initiation and revelation for him. After returning to New York, he began producing charcoal drawings, which he describes as "more real than anything done before, more free and immediate". All based on the sound of the explosions and vibrations, they are similar, in this respect, to the sketches he made during his childhood. "This was a revelation for me", the artist says, "because I was really feeling these drawings in my body. I knew that this experience was too important not to be carried forward". In this sense, his work develops a process of multisensorial simultaneity, a typical example of synaesthesia, which occurs when two different sensorial experiences coexist. Each of his paintings is the simultaneous combination of intuition and perception, drawing on visual memory, sounds, impressions, deep recollections, creative imagination and other sensations that all enter into play at the same moment:

"I can paint something starting from a memory, from an internal vibration which still lives deep inside me, or is generated by a sound I heard when I was a child [...] The way in which it came about was so real for me [...] The crater I painted during that trip to the beach appeared so suddenly that it connected immediately to my first memory of hearing bomb explosions and seeing craters in the ground. I remember that it all came pouring out so quickly that I used everything I could find – rags, spatulas, twigs or anything else – just to be able to convey that feeling I was experiencing of a distant memory".

This synesthetic connection between auditory and visual memory is present throughout Banisadr's work and seems to determine its formal construction. While the imaginary world he represents is highly personal and interior, the way it is formalized looks to the history of art. Standing in front of his work one can find iconographic sources ranging from Hieronymus Bosch to Francisco Goya and from Max Ernst to Willem de Kooning. All these references, ruminated and reworked at length, are combined with memories of Persian and Eastern art. Banisadr is also drawn to northern European landscape painting, featuring vivid contrasts of light and magnificent weather events: the whirl and flurry of the skies and vegetation. The sublimity of nature has unquestionably influenced many of his compositions, where the background and multiple planes seem to be traversed by gusts of winds, almost storms, that bring chaos and agitation into the painting. The artist's desire, however, is to transcend real data, verisimilitude, to arrive at the universal and the archetypical: "As a rule, I have always been interested in historical Renaissance paintings, because they are more allegorical, mythological, and do not refer to a particular time and place. I have never been a fan of 19th-century history paintings, ever since they became propagandistic and focussed on national histories, on a given time and place". In other words, though his paintings may sometimes appear grotesque, they steer clear of current affairs and comedy, going down the path of the surreal and the fantastical.

Banisadr's paintings are populated by an oneiric crowd consisting of dozens and dozens of figures, which seem to appear and disappear as if scraped and swept by a storm that drags those masses of bizarre and monstrous, grotesque and alien beings into an apocalyptic magma. It is a pandemonium, though the chaos is orderly, where the features of every creature inhabiting that universe do not correspond to recognizable and identifiable characters, as is the case in the pictorial tradition of the past. Banisadr's world is turbulent, on the brink of being swept away by a violent explosion, by a cataclysm – it is an apocalyptic reality. Everything is in motion and the different areas of the painting move at different speeds. Here the figures are rooted to the spot, there they vibrate frenetically, flying and crawling. Everything seems to be a scuffling scrum, becoming increasingly unreadable. There is something fascinating and confusing that defies objective description, and the subject seems both evanescent and mysterious. These compositions are captivating because they generate amazement as well as a strong sense of disquiet. They are like a symphony of high notes, reverberating and dissonant, which find a classical equilibrium thanks to a skilful organization of depth planes and the artist's tonal mastery, as well as the aforementioned synaesthetic care with which he distributes emphasis, without a main focus or a privileged point of view. The figurative core of the painting can be found simultaneously in various areas of the canvas, confusing depth and distance and impacting on time by creating a non-linear and non-hierarchical reading of the image.

What we see is like a bird's eye view. The eye is never directed to a single focal point, a single action, an emerging figure, while the richness and variety of anthropomorphic or naturalistic details is almost dizzying, like being on a carousel and seeing the world move on a single plane and begin to go out of focus due to speed. Hierarchies collapse. A multiplicity of ways of painting enriches the composition, making the reading of it more complex and varied through a constant play of revelations and diversions. Banisadr does not use geometric perspective to align the different elements at play according to importance. Pollock's dripping technique comes to mind here, although the way Banisadr works, with spatulas and brushes, is very different. Prevailing over the fury and excitement of dripping is the meticulous definition of figures and planes, with sophisticated outcomes reminiscent of miniaturist or calligraphic techniques. Besides Pollock, one can also think of Lee Krasner and Willem de Kooning, who certainly made a big impression on Banisadr when he arrived in the States. As did Hieronymus Bosch and Pieter Bruegel, despite obvious iconographic differences. Contrary to Florentine Renaissance painting, where geometry and mathematics define proportions and hierarchies of value, their paintings, like Banisadr's, have no fixed centre to serve as a basis for the perspectival grid or the distribution of figures and the organization of planes. In fact, as Ali Banisadr observes, in both Pollock and de Kooning's paintings the "composition is called 'all over' for this reason, because every part of the painting, every character included, every animal, tree, anything – all are equally important. There is no hierarchy. I find all this very interesting. Because one's eyes can move within the painting, and there is no way of finding a hierarchical character. All are equal, all share this energy within the painting". The succinct language, the foregoing of central perspective,

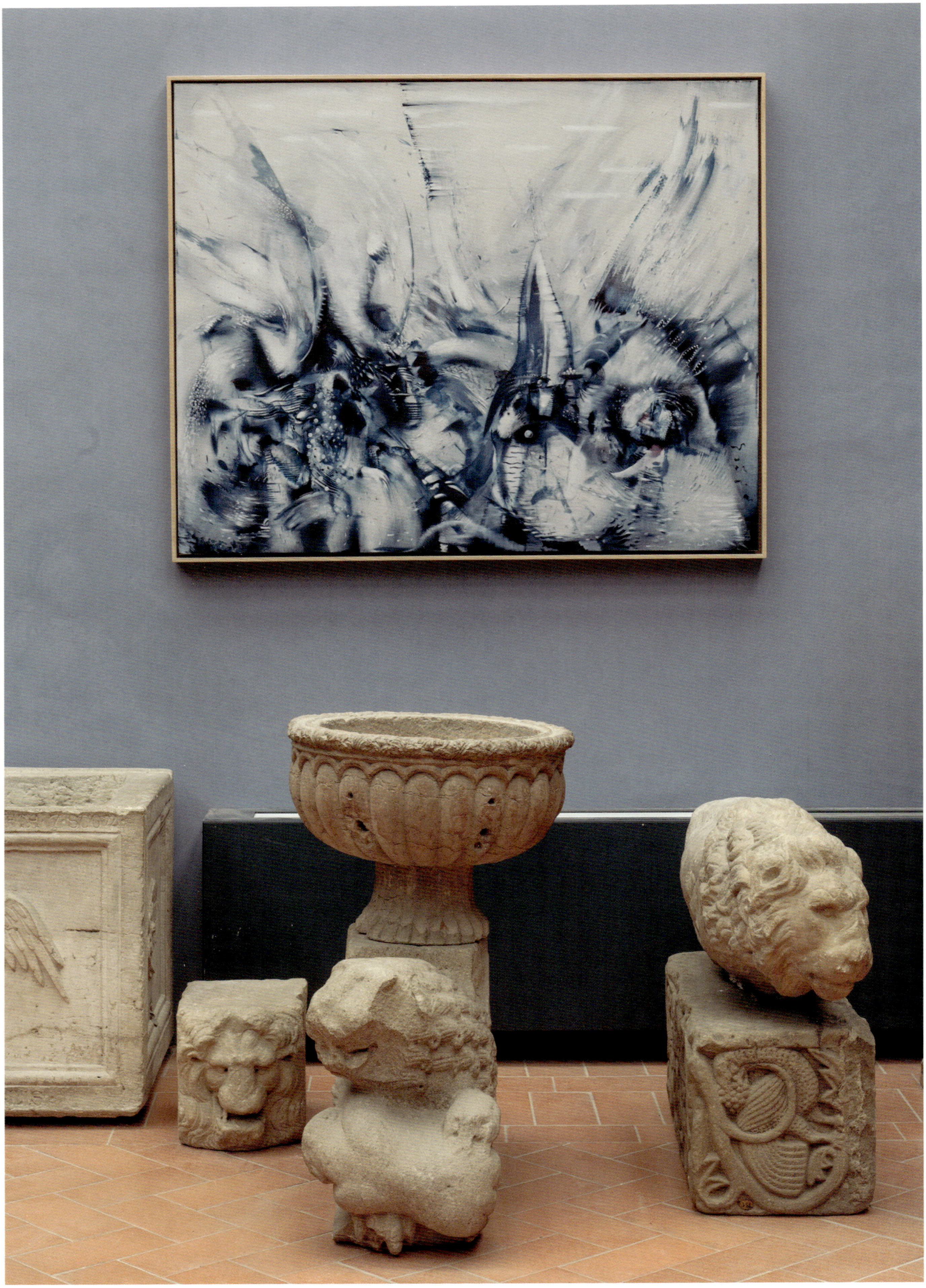

the sense of a polycentric composition where the recognizable references lose focus and retreat to the point of formlessness, remind us of how music, every genre of music, is important for Ali, and how listening to it always accompanies his imagining of a new painting.

Enticed by a surprising profusion of colors and planes, figurative and non-figurative elements, our gaze navigates within a kind of eccentric cosmogony that starts from the top and then moves down into a microcosm, animated by innumerable details. It is as if the carousel were slowing down and the gaze coming to rest on mysterious revelations, incomprehensible and improbable beings belonging to fantastical worlds, to the monstrous and otherworldly. We have the powerful sensation of witnessing an oneiric spectacle, of perceiving images as if in a dream, halfway between reality and the surreal. Fantastical bestiaries come to mind, grotesque and absurd, East-Asian landscapes where the rocks take on anthropomorphic forms or those of strange animals. The abstract and the figurative, the modernist idiom and medieval imaginary coexist in Banisadr's aesthetic experience. The agitated whirl of his canvases depicts a metamorphic world that draws on the past and the present – preserving and personalizing everything – offering us a timeless vision that is never limited to a closed cultural context, but is inspired by a synthesis of yesterday and today's art.

This way of working is one of the main reasons why Banisadr became so fascinated by Dante Alighieri and his great poem. The verses of the *Divine Comedy* also give readers access to an entire new world. Dante – remarks Banisadr, a passionate reader of the Florentine poet – included characters from mythology and epic poems, historical and political figures from his own times, metaphysical and popular beings. In some sections of the *Inferno*, apocalyptic scenarios also become real, reflecting everyday life. It is a synthetic poem – a pandemonium that made a powerful impression on Banisadr. And this multitude of characters contributed to creating the visionary world that we all know – a universal encyclopaedia of knowledge. "When I immersed myself in Dante's *Inferno*, a whole world opened up from his verses", the artist declares. "Dante gathered numerous fragments of knowledge taken from old epic poems, from mythology, from history and from politics to produce a visionary masterpiece. I am fascinated by these multidimensional worlds in which the poet brings together a whole universal encyclopaedia of knowledge. I am also fascinated by how many figures can coexist within a single person, because, psychologically speaking, all the characters that Dante encounters in the *Inferno* are in a certain sense the voices and ideas of the very characters that reverberate through his mind".

Beautiful Lies is one of the works inspired by Dante on show in the Palazzo Vecchio's Sala dei Gigli, opposite Donatello's *Judith and Holofernes*, and it was chosen as the title for the whole exhibition. The 'beautiful lie', beneath which the truth is concealed, is an expression that Dante used

Rhizome
Museo
Stefano Bardini

to speak of his works and of allegorical poems in general. It is also perfectly suited to Banisadr's work, which, with its energetic marks and colors ranging from the psychedelic to the monochrome, stage his private world (and a universal one) of violence and isolation, anguish and marvel, but also of memory and longing. "I think that collective memory is something very deep inside ourselves", says the artist. "It is something in the public domain, which we can all access. I am sure that Dante too drew from this source and I like the way the narrative develops, bringing the protagonists further and further down into the earth. To me, this is a metaphor for the personal journey we must take, deep within ourselves, to discover what is hidden inside us. This is the place, intimate and profound, where I always go to find symbols with which to express myself in my paintings".

It Was Written
Museo
Stefano Bardini

Pages 18-19:
Ordered Disorders 1
Museo
Stefano Bardini

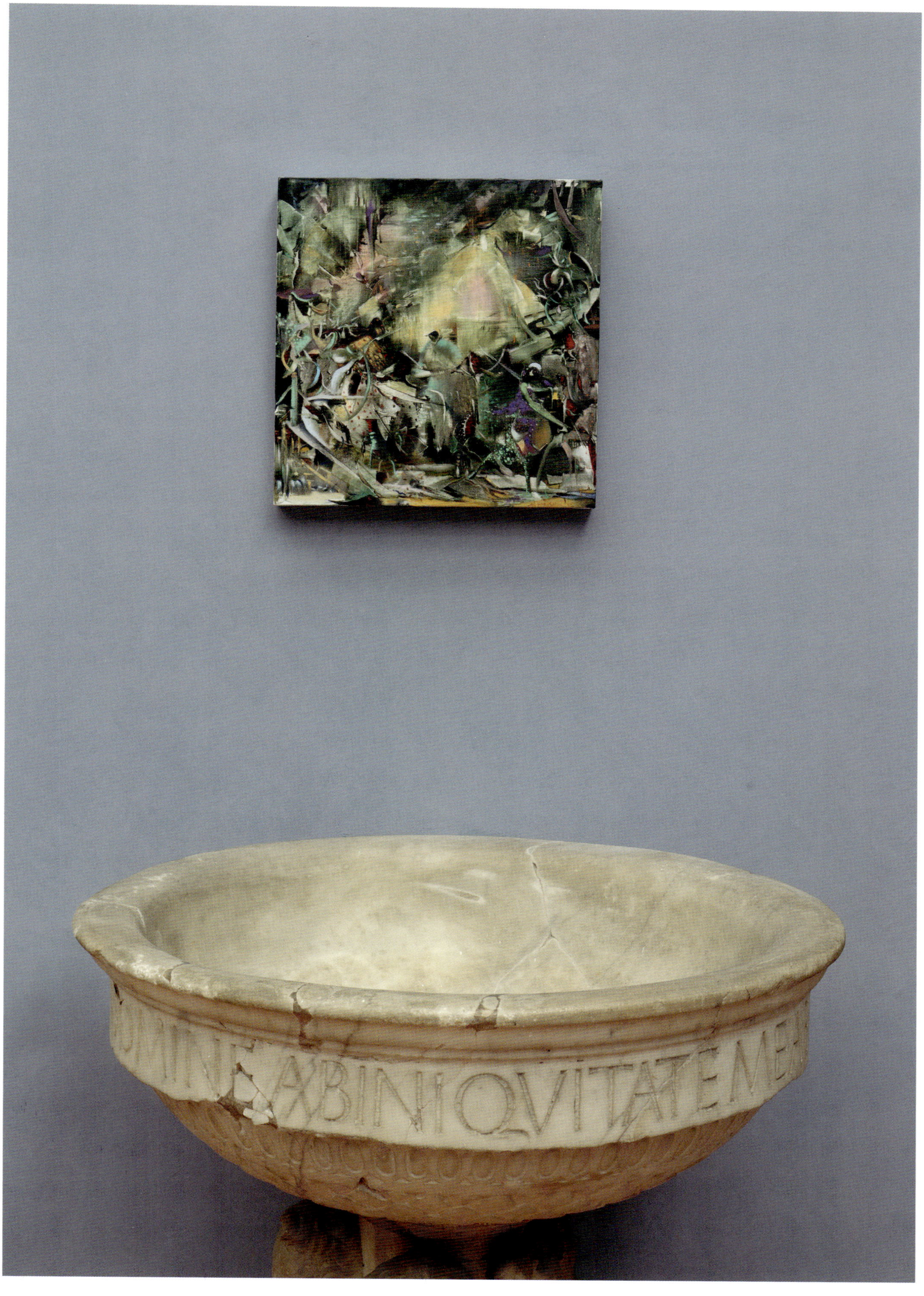
OMINE ABINIQVITATE ME

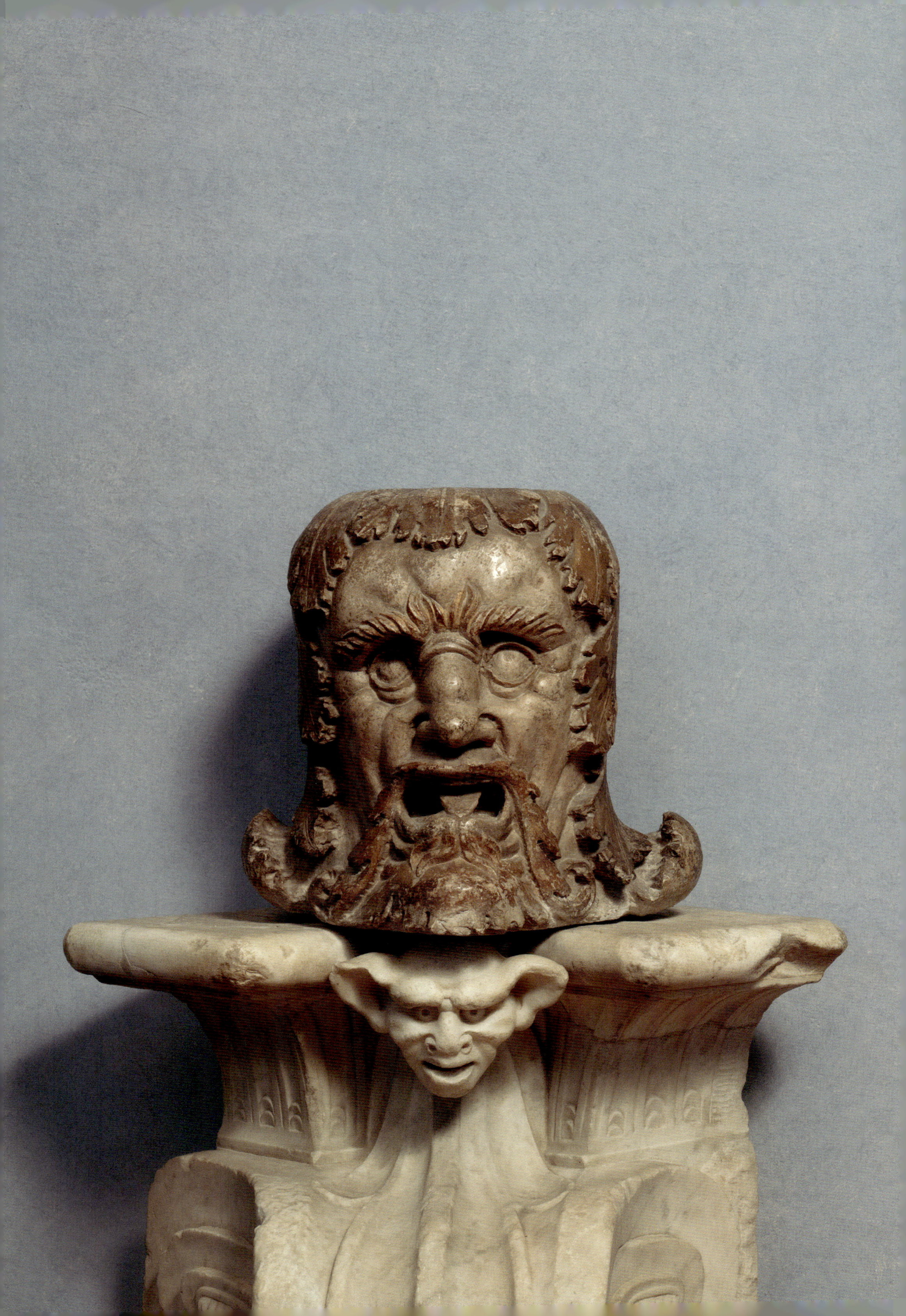

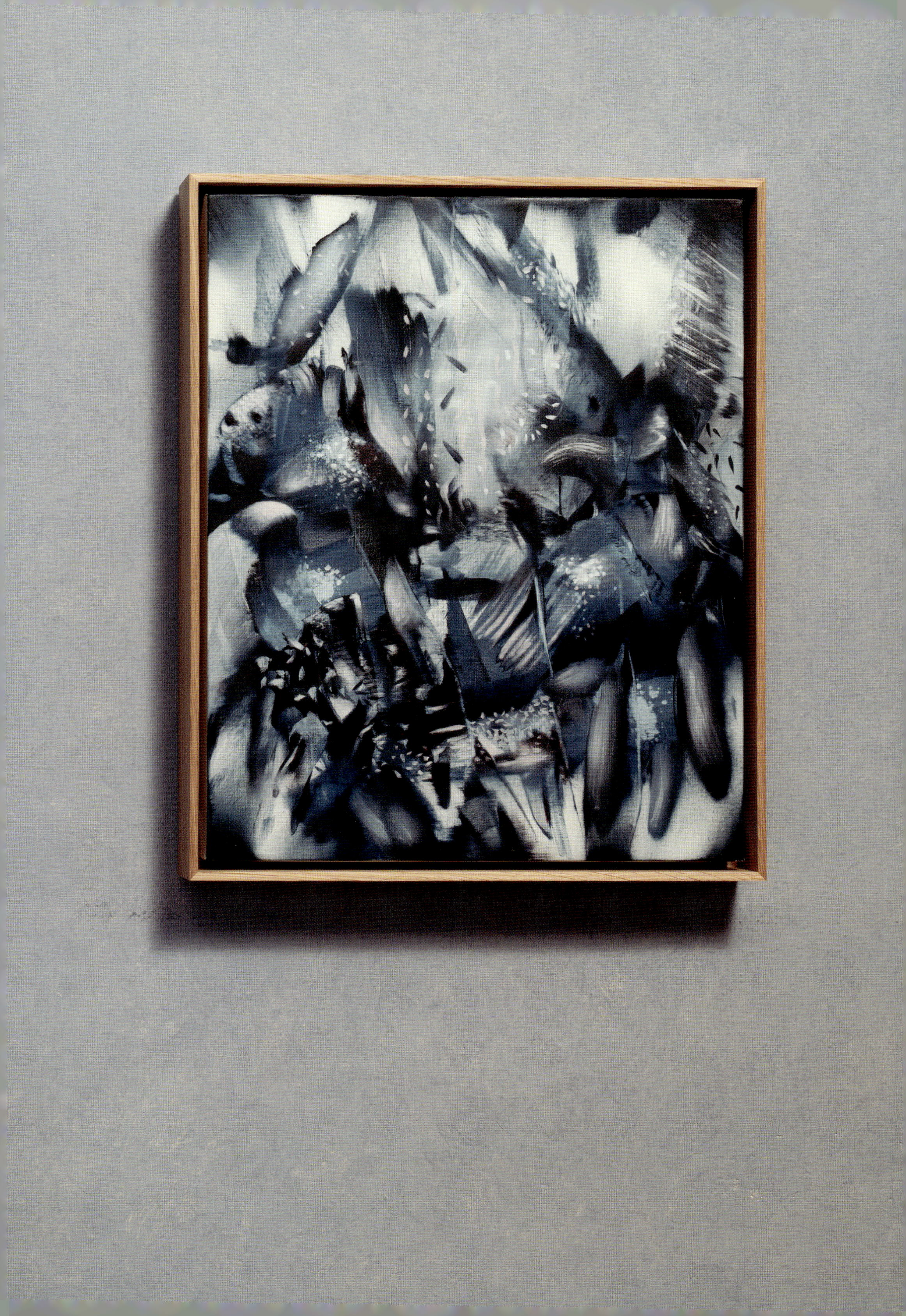

ALI BANISADR AND DANTE ALIGHIERI: PAINTER-POET AND POET-PAINTER

Mary Jo Bang

A poem is a talking painting, a painting is a silent poem.
Simonides of Ceos, 556-468 BCE

Like Dante in his *Inferno*, and like Hieronymus Bosch in that triptych referred to today as *The Garden of Earthly Delights*, Ali Banisadr has created a set of imaginary landscapes peopled with figures that gesture to myriad sorts of human mischief and the calamities that await the bad actors. If there seem to be fewer overt narrative details in Banisadr's paintings than what readers find in Dante's Cantos (or in Bosch's *Garden*), it might be worth remembering that we have no 'likeness' of Dante's imaginative world outside of his words. Much later, Sandro Botticelli, Gustave Doré, John Flaxman, and William Blake would 'translate' Dante's text into visual images but who's to say whether Dante's mental images would match those recreations. The fact is, any renderings that allude to Dante's *Inferno* are necessarily based on an artist's singular interpretation. The resulting works will invariably echo the artist's historical moment, if only in the raw materials, the artist's biographical details, and possibly even something incidental the artist saw on the street that day, or the day before, or five years earlier.

The beginning of any work of art involves a moment not unlike the moment of Dante's 'coming to' in "una selva oscura" (a dark forest) in the *Inferno*. In Italian, *oscura* most often means dark, however, depending on context, it can, like its English cognate 'obscure', mean unclear, ambiguous, or difficult to fathom. In his painting *Beautiful Lies*, Banisadr captures the psychological sense of "una selva oscura" far better than an artist who would present us with a reductive idea of a dim-lit woodland with leaves and trees. The dislocation one finds in the Banisadr painting is a more apt equivalent for the character Dante's state of mind, that experience of being so utterly lost one is about to give up. In the painting, left of center, there is the suggestion of a figure astride a beast. The red sleeves gesture to the red robe the poet Dante is often pictured wearing. And yet this figure has polka-dot pants and wears a wizard's hat. If this is Dante, and the beast he's riding the lion or spotted leopard the character encounters as he attempts to escape the forest in Canto I, it would seem that Dante has tamed the beast. Of course, overcoming one's weaknesses is exactly what the hero must do in order to escape the vexed state of mind threatening to undo him so that he can begin the journey toward redemption. If we like, we can also imagine the figure as the painter himself, perhaps with a Prince Valiant haircut, who has had to conquer his own hesitation in the face of the blank canvas.

In Banisadr's *Inferno* paintings, fragmentation and suggestion give a sense of myriad possibilities – as opposed to any sense of completion that

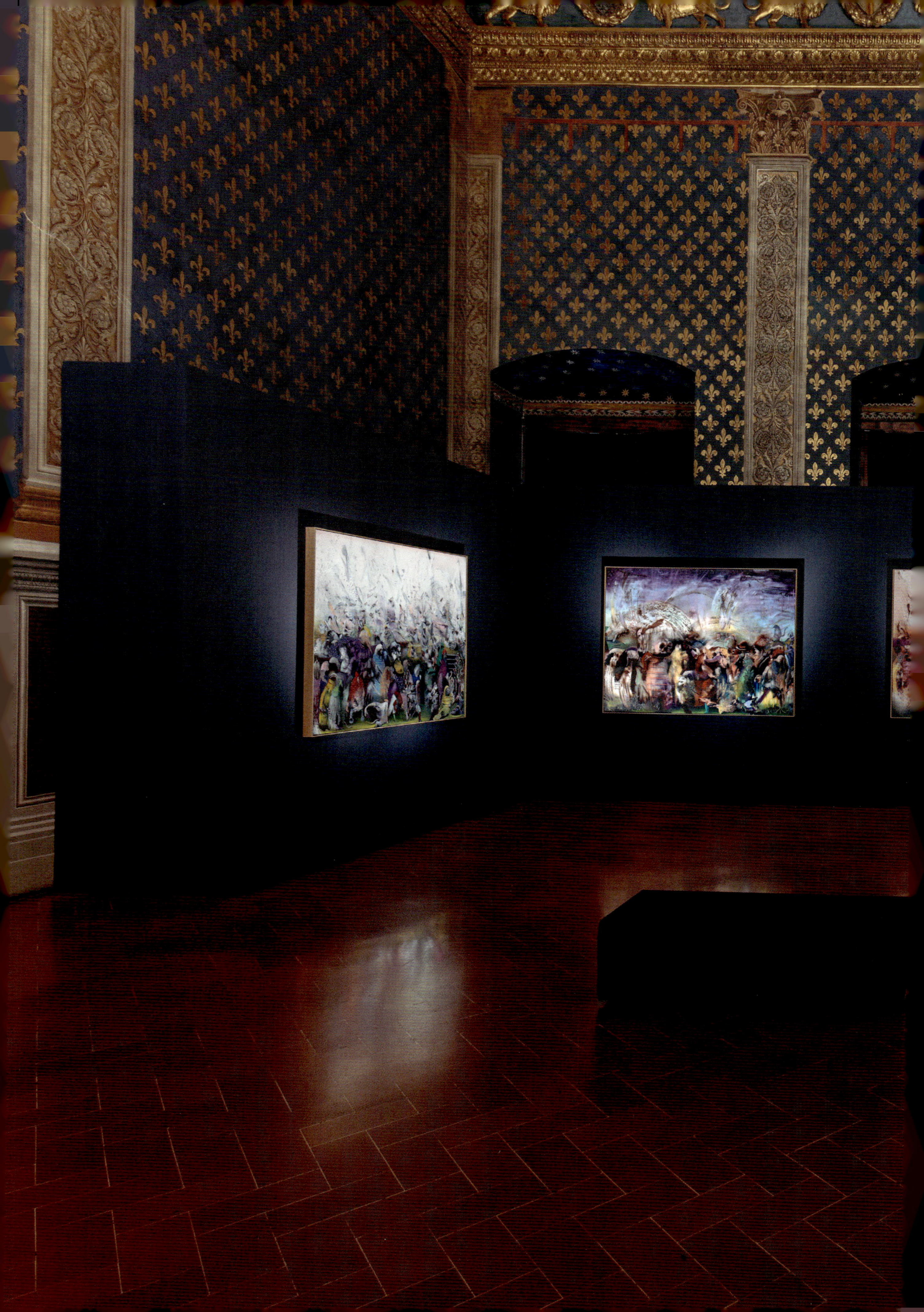

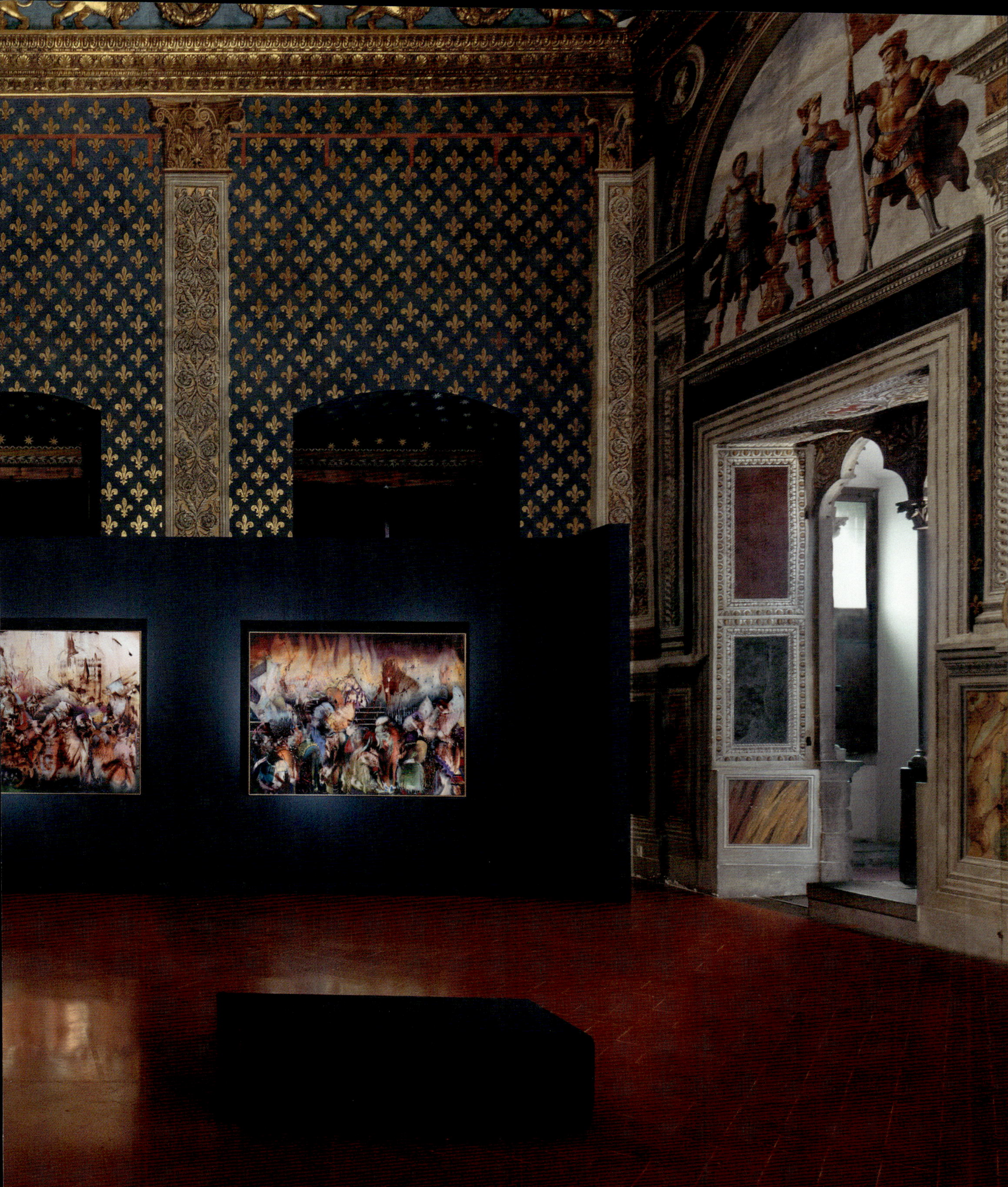

might limit possible reading. This indeterminacy brilliantly tracks the ever-restless mind. The paintings become representations of webs of thought so intricate they can't be unraveled. This is exactly what poetry does. The poet exploits the natural ambiguity of words to mean multiple things so as to push the reader's mind in various directions at once and thereby expand the realm of the poem from the literal to the much more expansive figurative. Banisadr is working precisely as Dante worked. Dante used the elements of poetry – patterning, word choice, line breaks, stanza breaks, phonic echoes – as the basis of a figurative allegory that addresses what it is to engage in the struggle to be worthy of love. The lion isn't only a lion but is a signifier of the sin of pride; the leopard stands for the sin of excessive lust; the she-wolf, the sin of greed. These traits hold us back from being generous and achieving dignity. Dante told his story in a radically new way, including inventing his own interlocking rhyme scheme. Similarly, Banisadr has used every brushstroke not to illustrate a story that has already been told but to instead, create glimpses through plate glass windows into rooms where the elements of Dante's story keep collapsing on top of one another.

Banisadr's *Inferno* paintings trigger memories not only of the original version of *Inferno*, but the story as it has passed through time and been translated again and again into English. The result of this visual upheaval is that we viewers are also wandering across the canvas. We might be Dante in the forest, or perhaps even Alice in Wonderland. Both Dante and Alice are continually being forced to make something of the strange sights they see. The teeth in the lower right-hand corner of *Beautiful Lies* might belong to one of Dante's adversaries at the edge of the forest – the leopard, lion, or she-wolf – but the sense of a toothy grin might also take us to the wiseacre Cheshire Cat who tells Alice, "Imagination is the only weapon in the war with reality". The creature wearing these teeth has something about it that seems both human (the minimal impression of clothes) and totally cartoonish (the bulbous head). This is true of all of Banisadr's creatures and that makes them a perfect fit for those we find in the *Inferno* where each figure we meet, from Greek and Roman myth, Tuscan politics, or the Catholic Bible, is a larger-than-life caricature of human error. Banisadr's figures are caught between imagination and reality, between the sinners one meets in the *Inferno* and comic-book characters.

In *Underworld*, the second *Inferno*-inspired Banisadr's painting, one intuits a darkening palate. The darkness matches the fact that the lower Dante and Virgil descend, the darker the air – this to signify that the farther one is from divine love, the less one can see their way clear. As he and Virgil approach the 9th circle, where a three-headed Satan is eternally locked in a lake of ice, the miasma is so thick and the air so dark Dante mistakes chained giants for towers. Similarly, the viewer of the painting has to participate in the construction of a narrative by resolving puzzling shapes and interrupted lines. The clearest figure in the painting can be found in the lower right-hand corner where a figure (Dante? Banisadr?) appears to be walking away, toward the left, which is the path one must take to canvas the circles of hell.

The sense of sinister forces becomes even more apparent in the third Dante-indebted painting, *SOS*. SOS is that Morse-code distress signal that gets misunderstood as an acronym of "Save Our Souls". A fiery conflagration – which echoes the boiling river of blood in the 7th circle, where violence is punished, and the tongues of flame that hide Ulysses and Diomedes in the eighth pit of the 8th circle, where one pays for the sin of having persuaded others to act against their own self-interest – covers the entire width of the painting. The shooting flames appear to be behind what could be barbed-wire fencing. Woven into the foreground, talons, teeth, and veiled figures, all of which takes us to other moments in the *Inferno*. The veils – and the flames – might also take us to the painter's homeland, Iran. The spiked green tail brings Geryon on stage, that winged fraudster with the face of an affable man, lion claws, and a scorpion's tail, that carries Virgil and Dante on his back down to the otherwise inaccessible 8th circle, where varied types of deception each receive a uniquely suitable punishment.

Social critique is fundamental to the work of both Dante and Banisadr. The *Inferno* is a stinging indictment of the rampant corruption in both the medieval Church and the fractured State, which directly involved Dante. Betrayed by Pope Boniface VIII and by members of his own political party, he was tried *in abstentia* on false charges and exiled from Florence, to be burnt at the stake if he returned. Instead of limiting himself to recriminations for these specific treacheries, Dante laments all human behaviors that destroy the personal connections that bind societies together. At the entrance to Hell, between Limbo and the River Acheron, across which Charon ferries the sinners, he describes an antechamber for those who, although not guilty of one of the seven deadly sins, lacked the courage to stand up for right when they were given the opportunity. This area is populated by hordes chasing an ever-shifting banner. Banisadr likewise gestures, in the desperation of the title (*SOS*), toward our own dire moment of rampant political duplicity, incivility, xenophobia, disinformation, envy, and greed. One can read these urgent concerns in the tumult of the scene: the disordered margin between the fire and the foreground, the gold chain, the hoods, the rough-sketch grotesquery of an upside-down orange head being eaten by a spiny creature – not unlike the indelible image of Ugolino in the *Inferno*. Deceived, imprisoned, and then starved to death alongside his sons and grandsons, now sentenced to the 9th circle for his own sins, he ceaselessly gnaws on the head of his torturer, Archbishop Ruggieri.

In each of these three canvases, elements of Dante's durable story, having now lasted 700 years from the date of his death – keep crashing against the

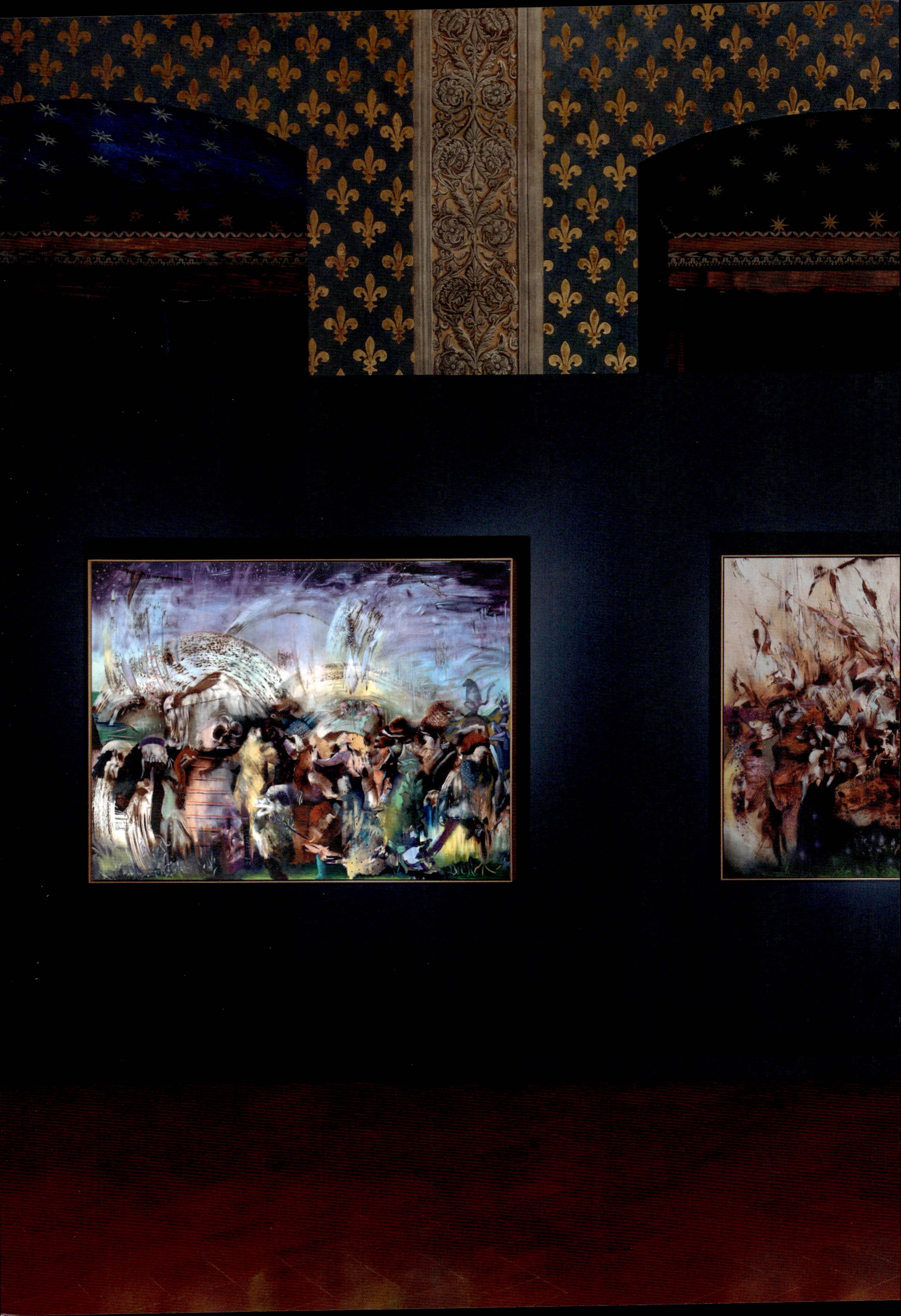

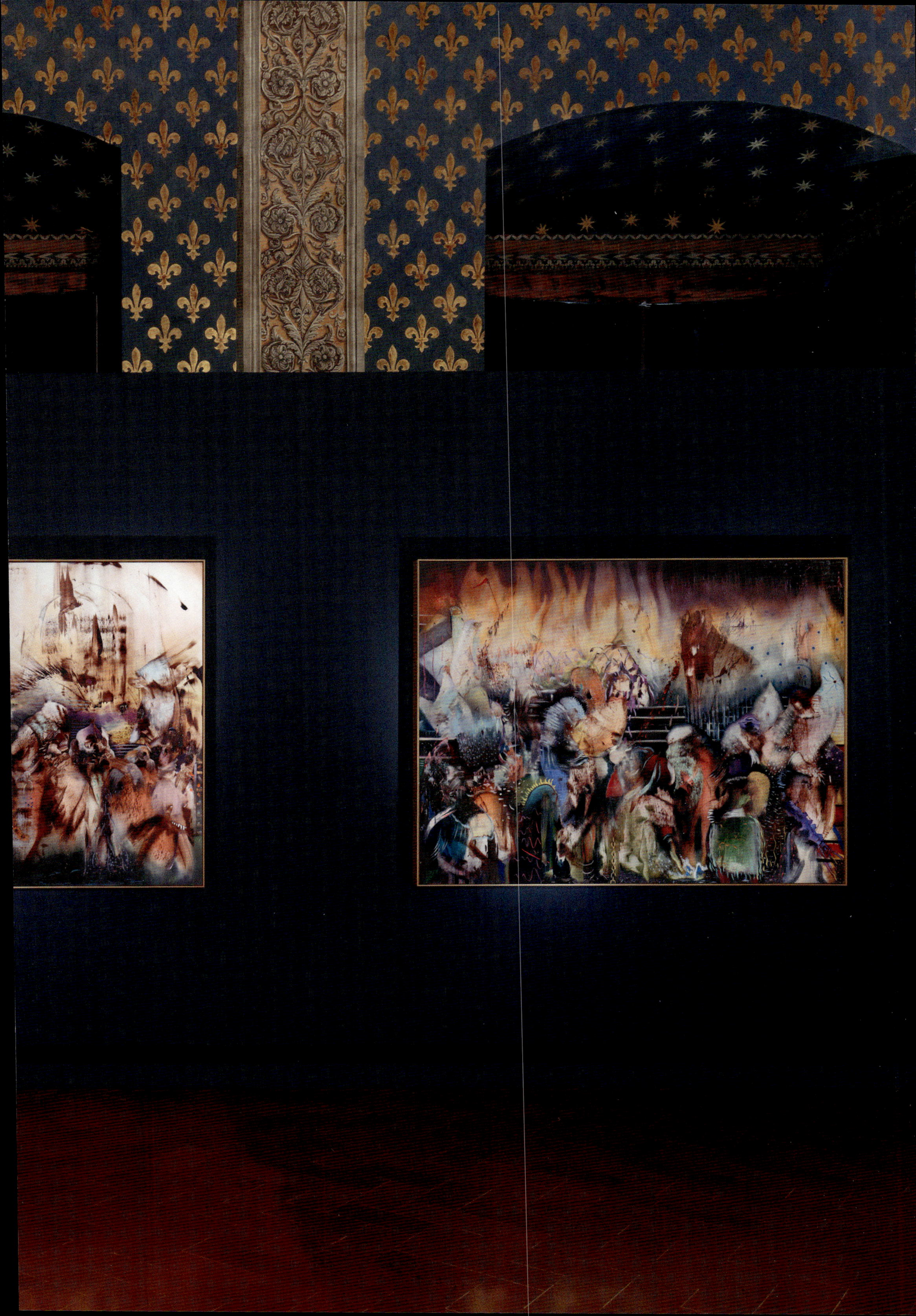

instability of passing time and shifting geographies, all the while being further complicated by the mind's never-ending attempt to fathom what it is to be human. In *Inferno*, Virgil, playing the role of Reason, acts as a guide for the bewildered Dante. In Banisadr's paintings, an equally Dantean hell of displacement and estrangement, Dante's *Inferno* acts as the guide, helping us find our way through a disquieting landscape that is stunningly gorgeous and wondrously fascinating.

Pages 22-23 / 26-27:
Paintings set-up in
the Sala dei Gigli,
Palazzo Vecchio

The Devil,
Canto 28
Sala dei Gigli,
Palazzo Vecchio

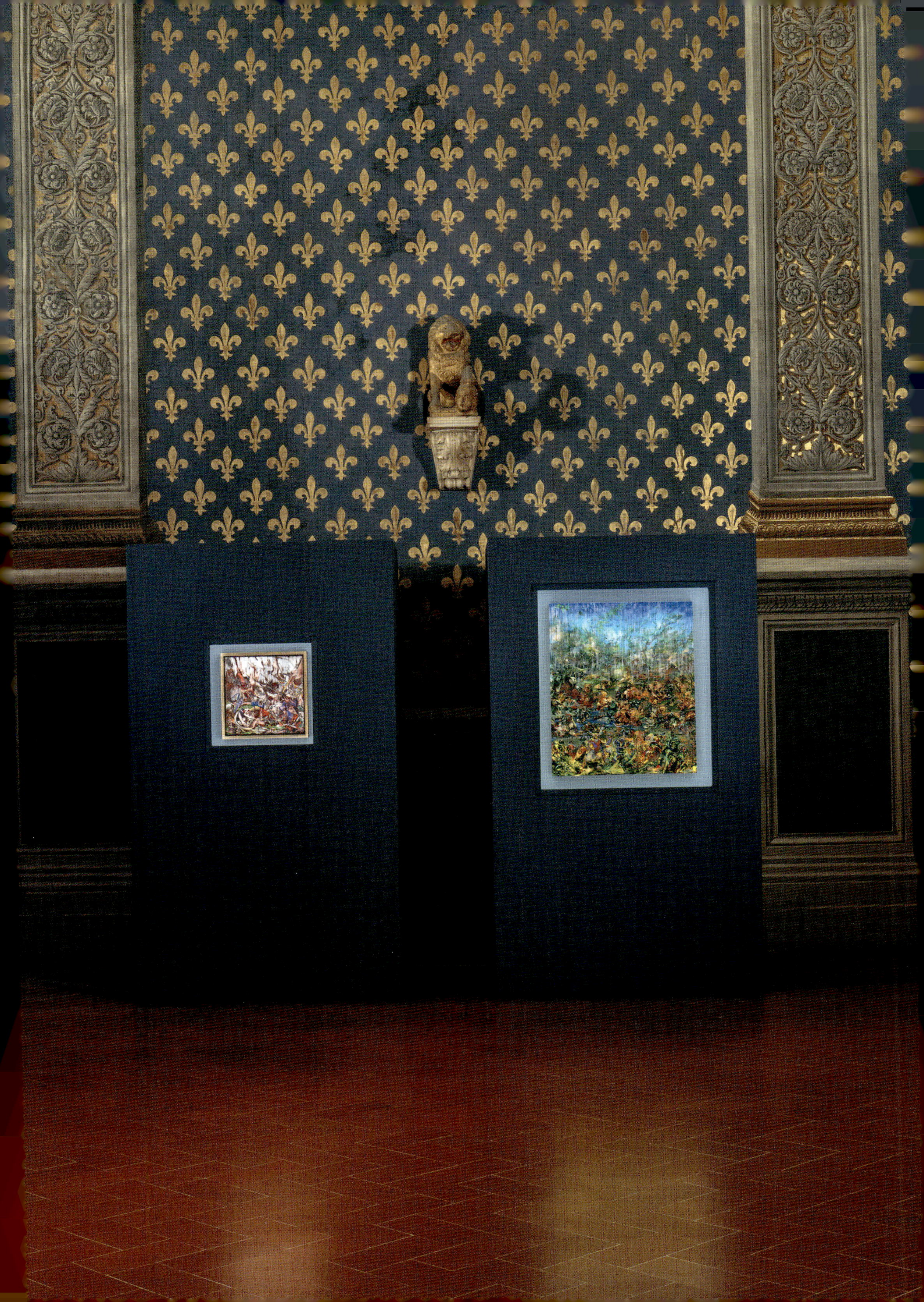

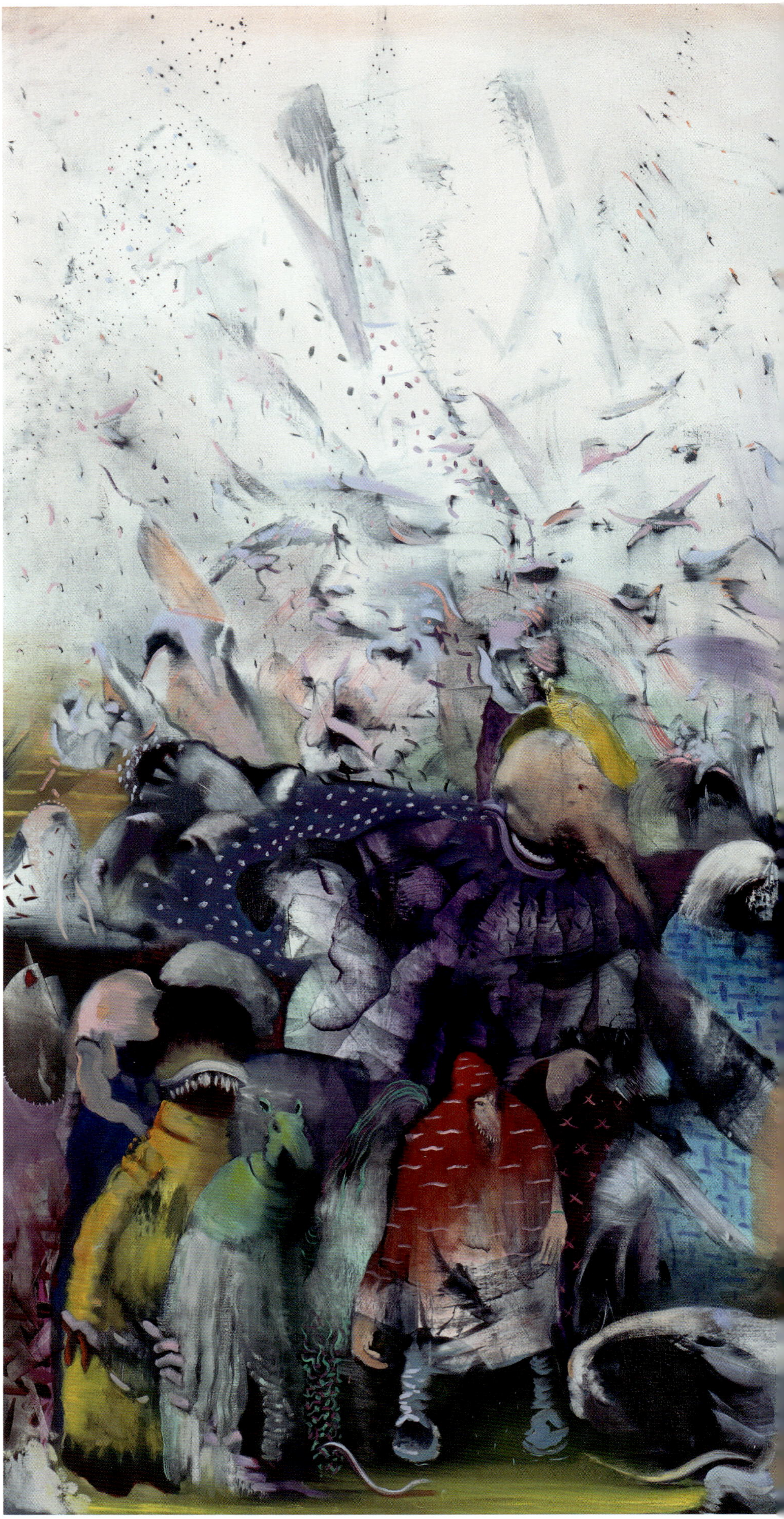

The Rise of the Blond
2016
Oil on linen
167.6 x 223.5 cm
Private collection,
Milan

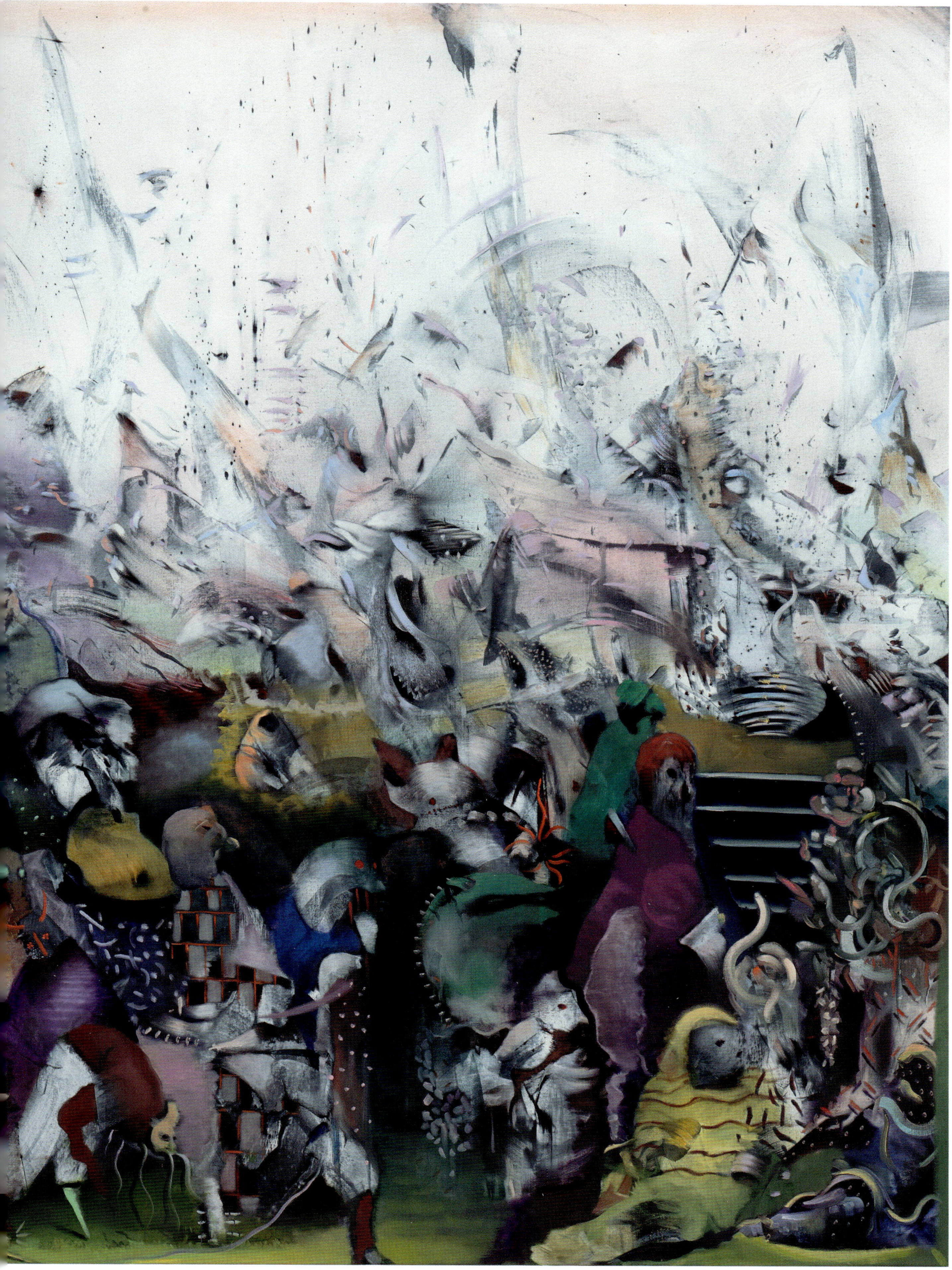

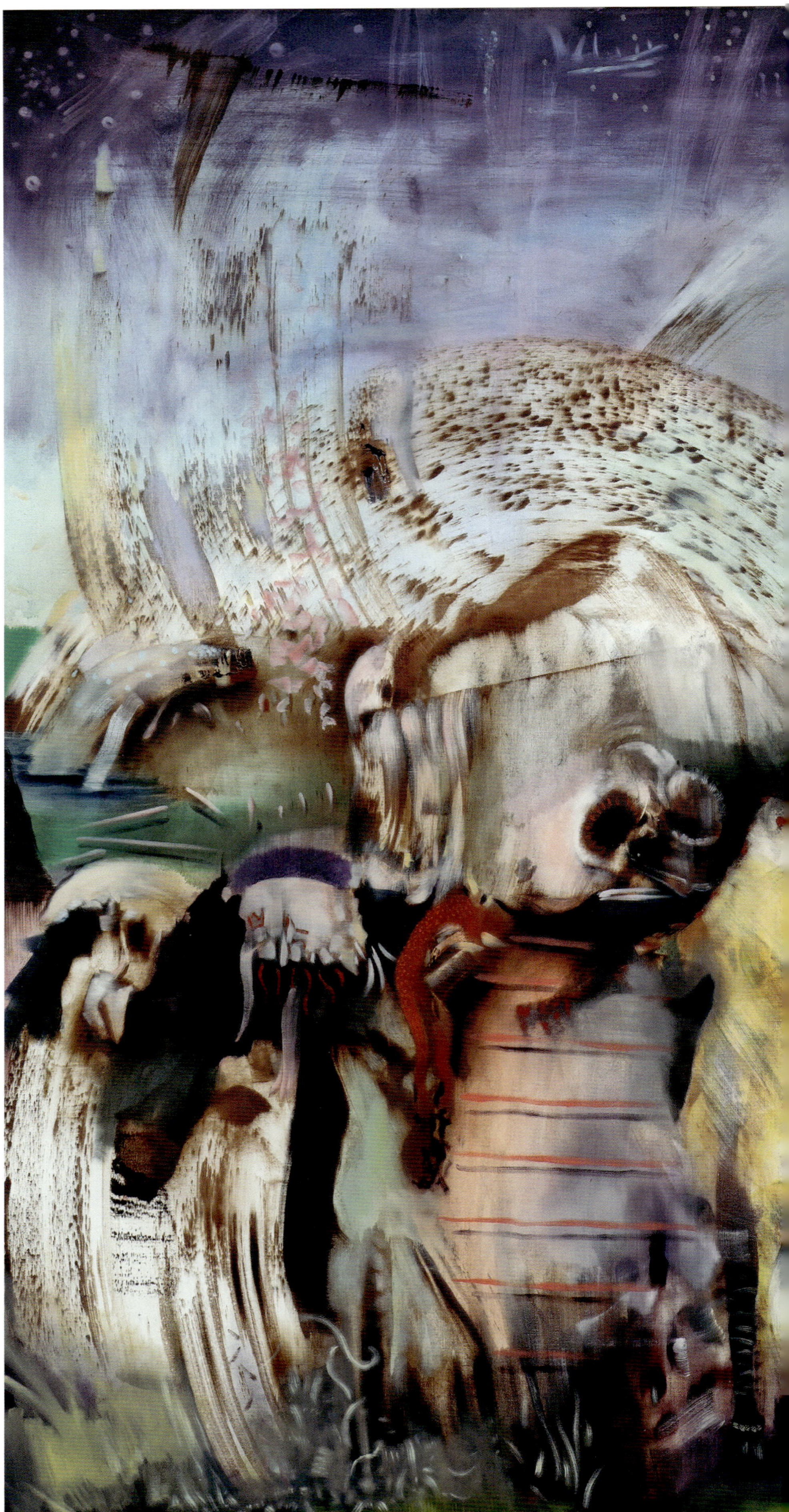

Underworld
2021
Oil on linen
167.6 x 223.5 cm
Courtesy Thaddaeus
Ropac, London,
Paris, Salzburg

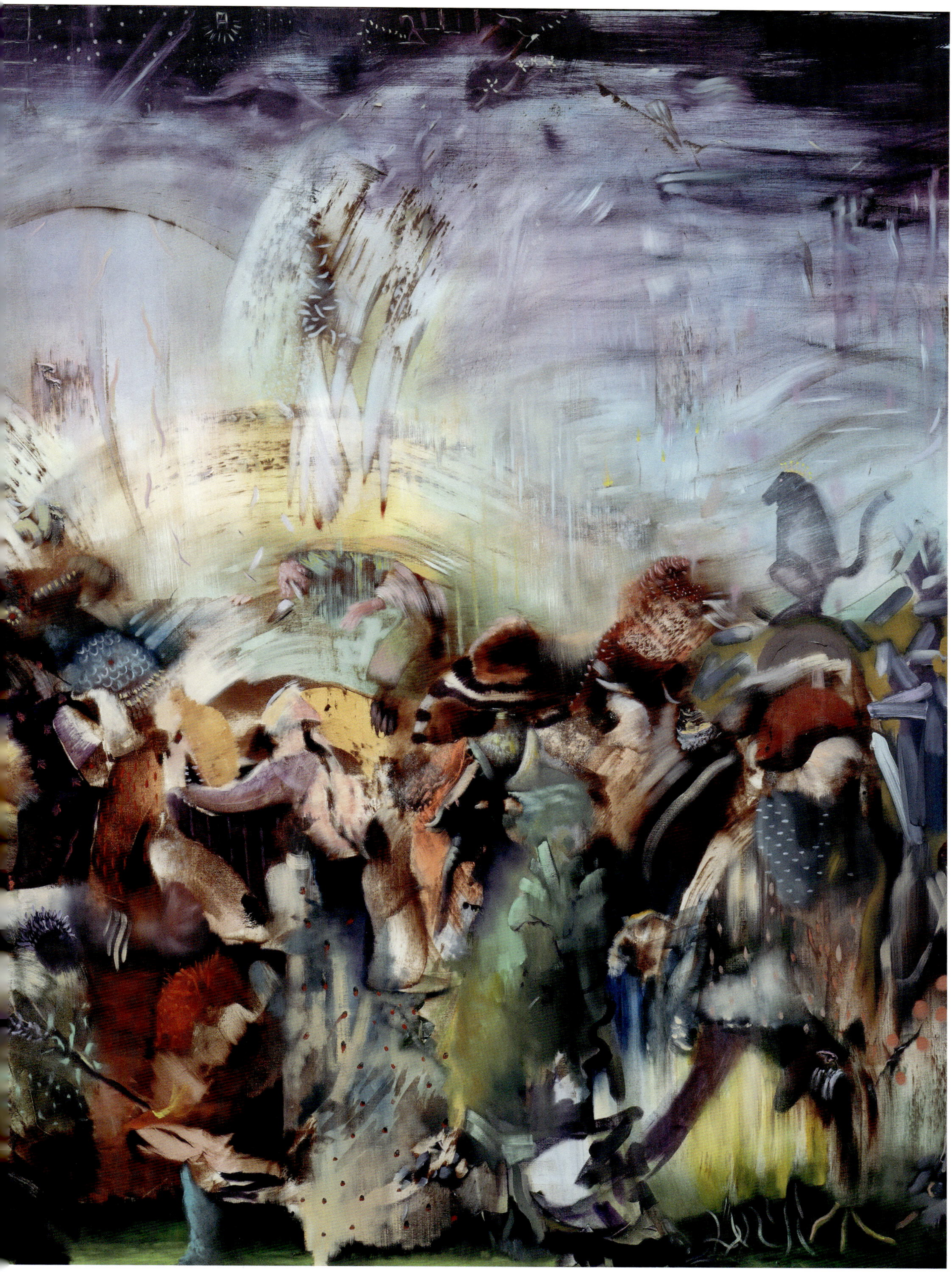

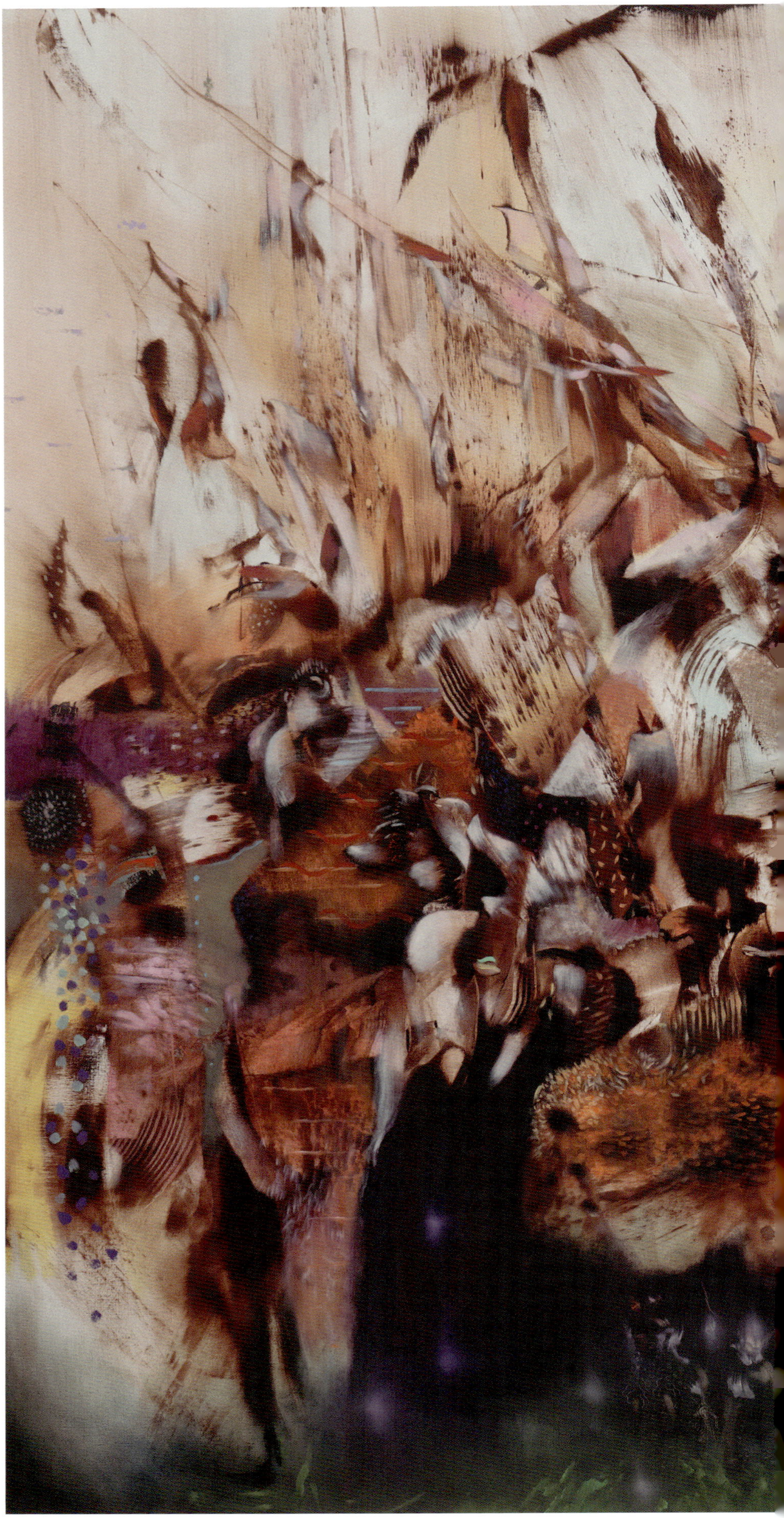

Beautiful Lies
2021
Oil on linen
167.6 x 223.5 cm
Courtesy Thaddaeus Ropac, London, Paris, Salzburg

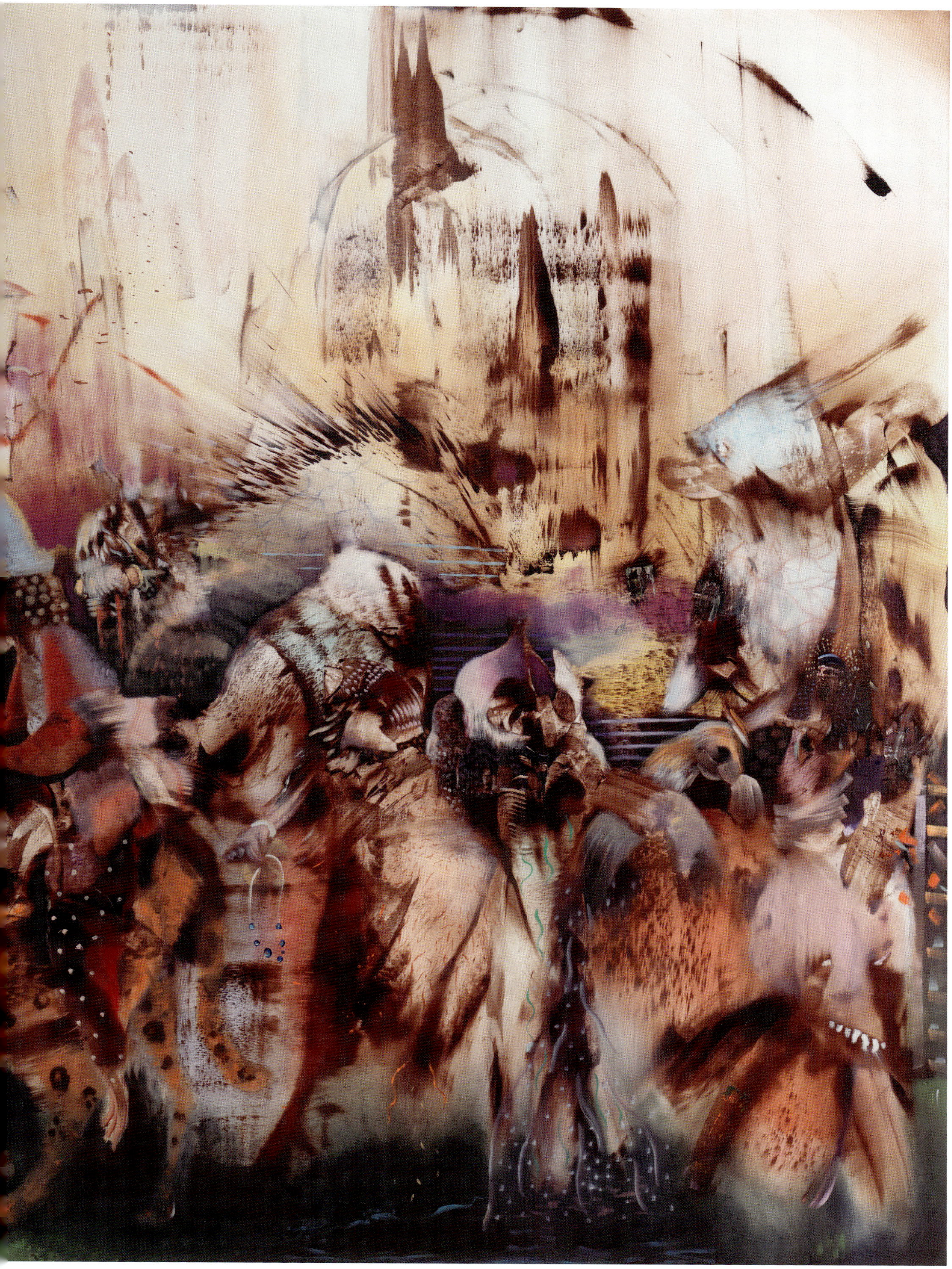

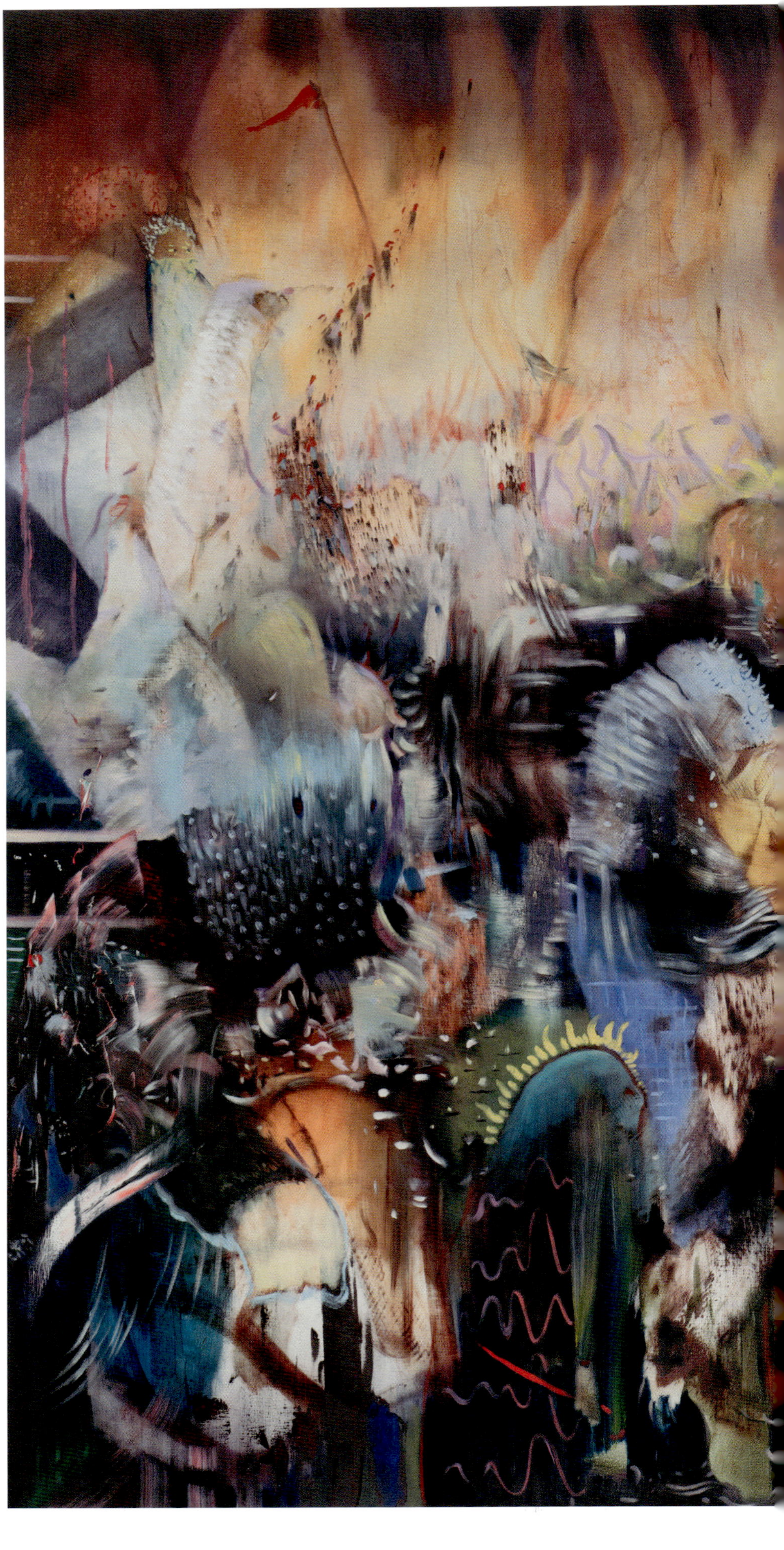

SOS
2020
Oil on linen
167.6 x 223.5 cm
Private collection

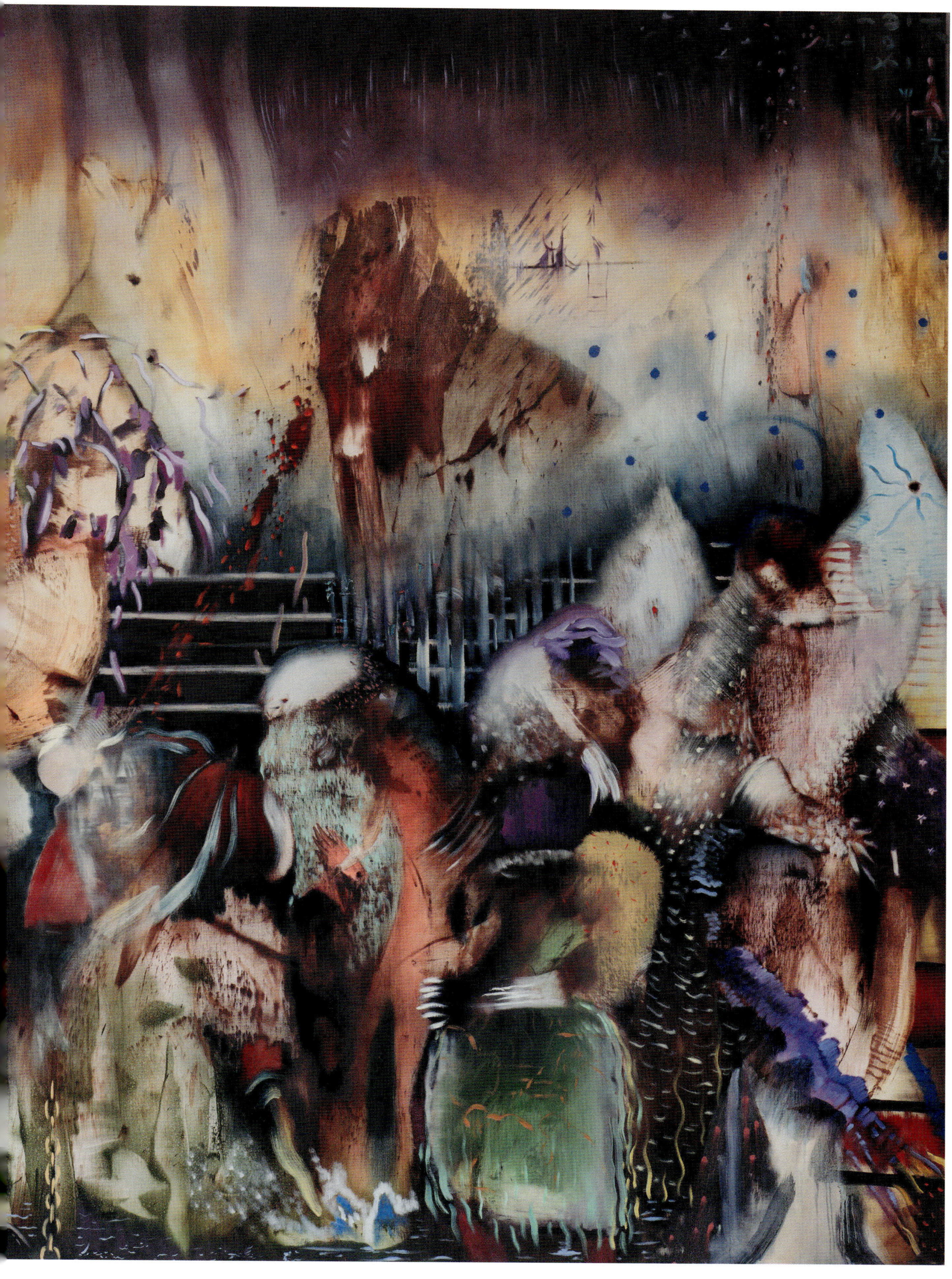

Canto 28
2011
Oil on linen
91.4 x 76.2 cm
Private collection,
Brescia

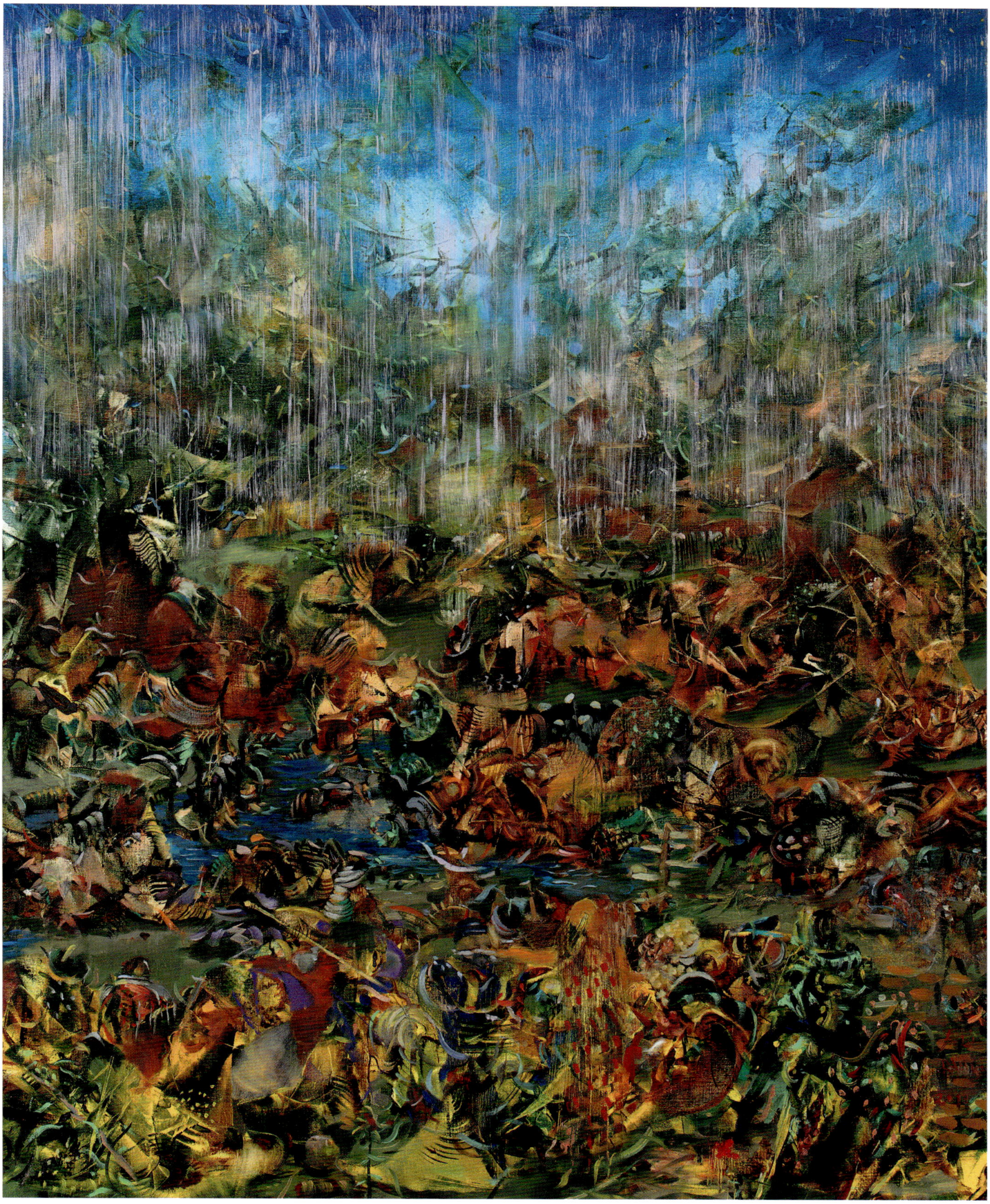

The Devil
2012
Oil on linen
40.6 x 40.6 cm
Private collection,
London

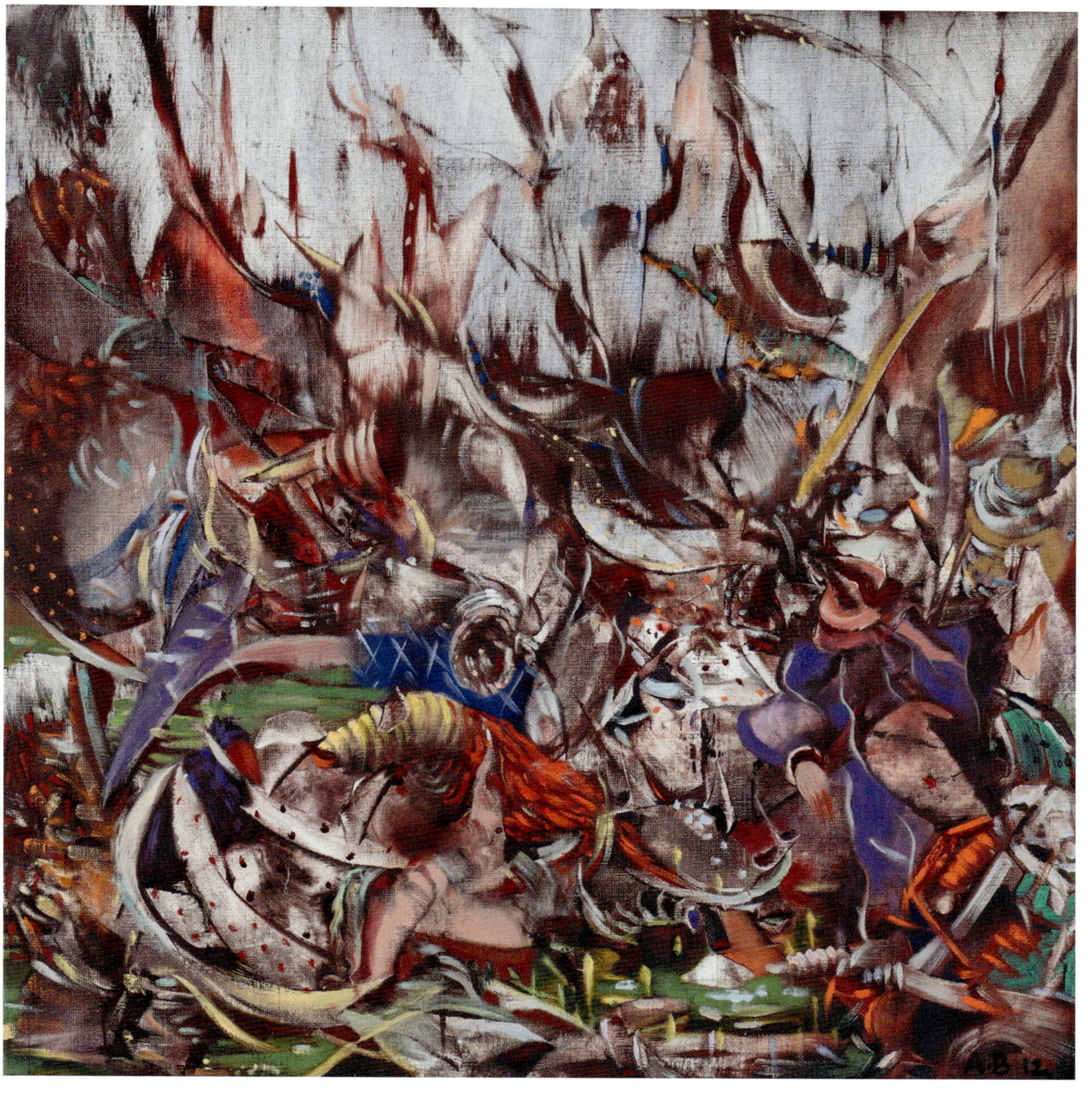

It Was Written
2012
Oil on linen
40.6 x 40.6 cm
Private collection,
Milan

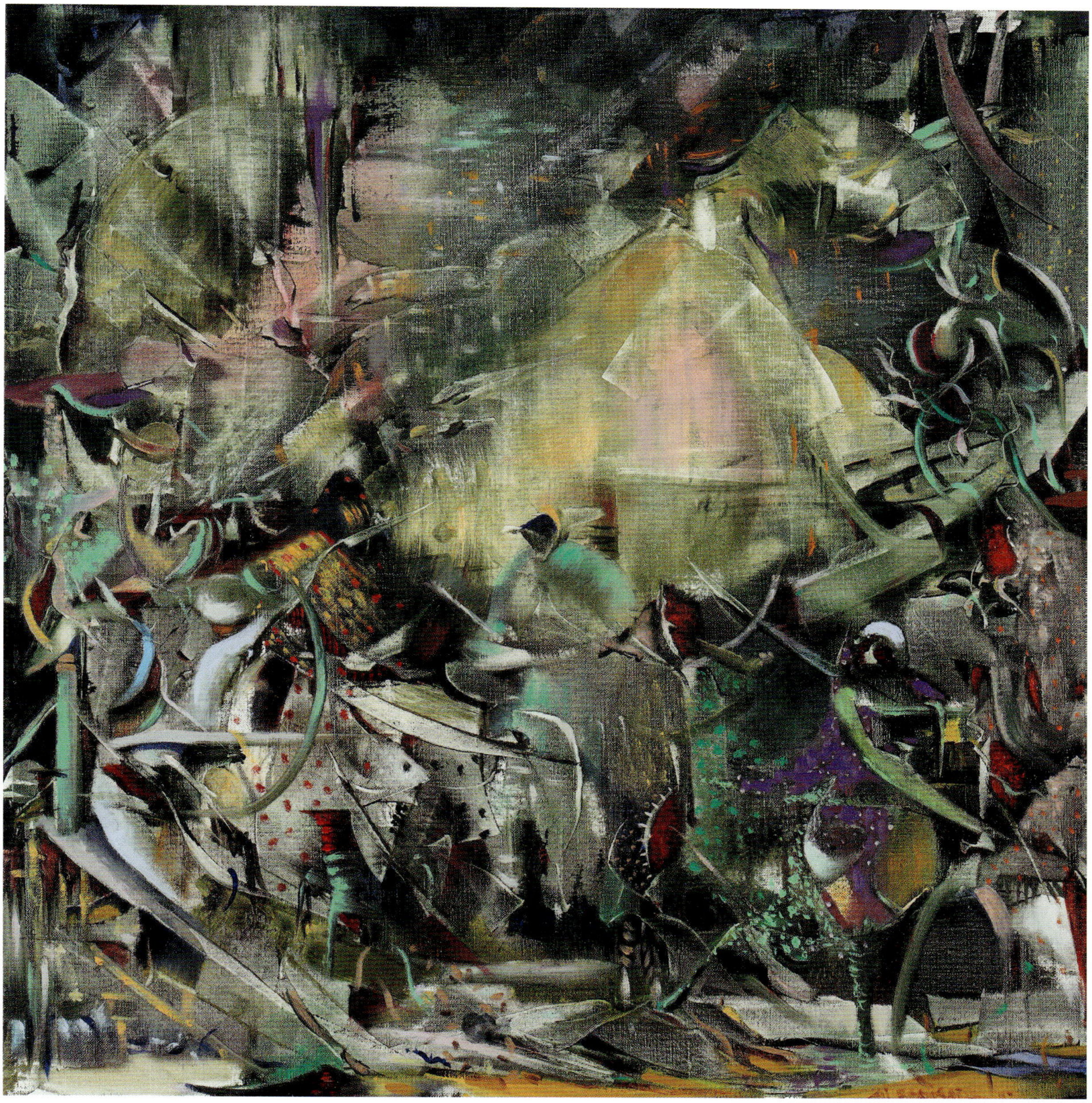

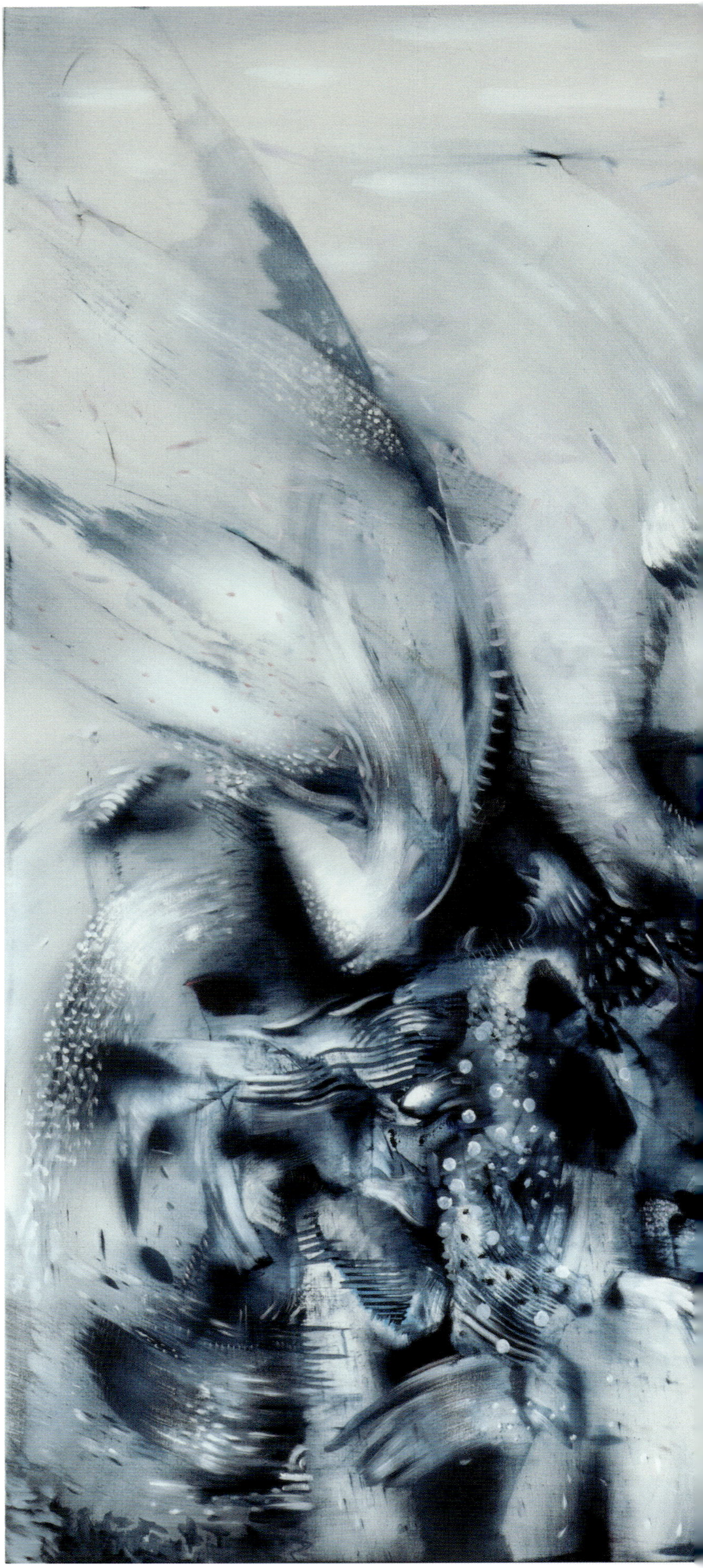

Rhizome
2019
Oil on linen
121.9 x 152.4 cm
Sera Han collection

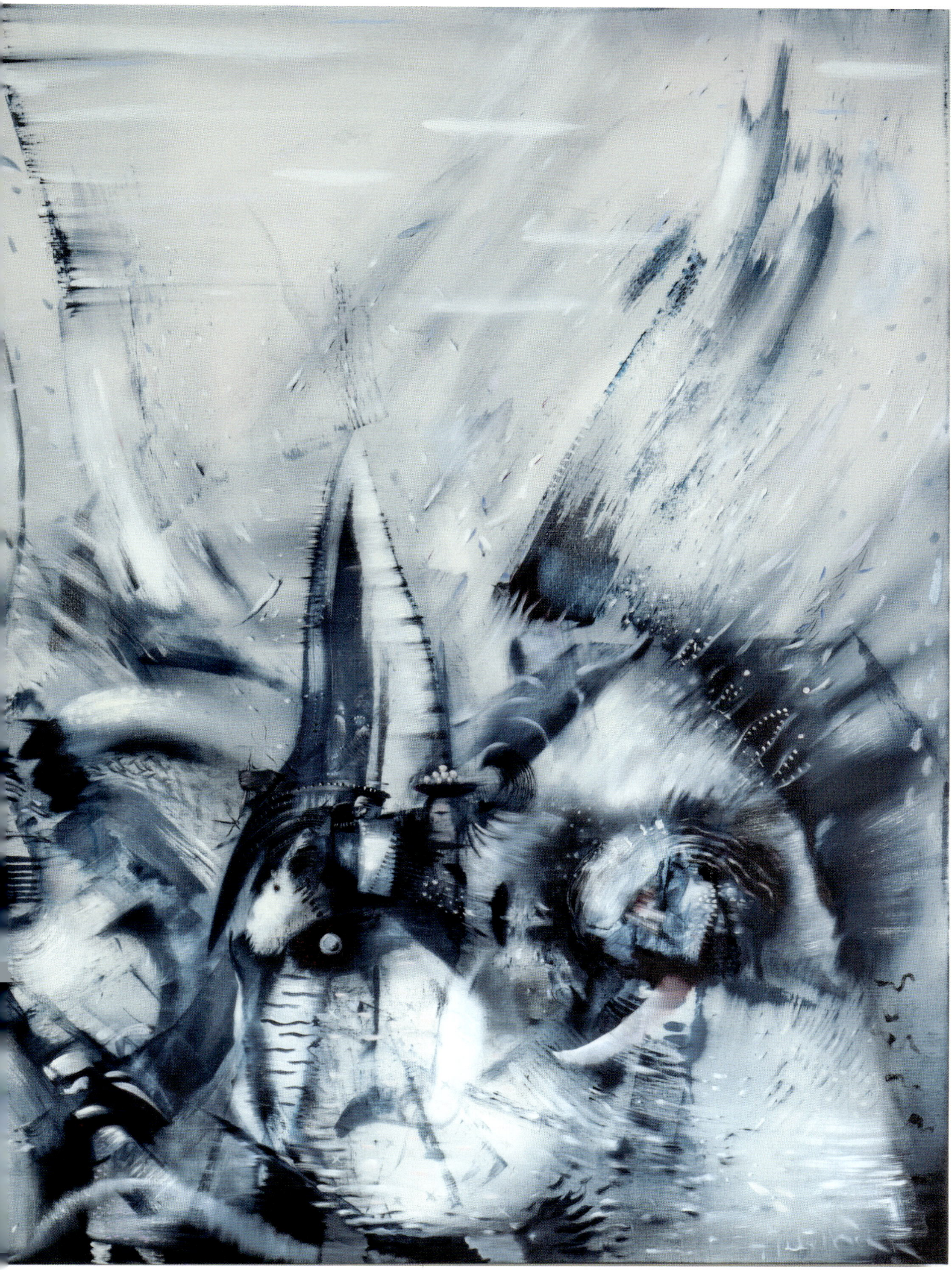

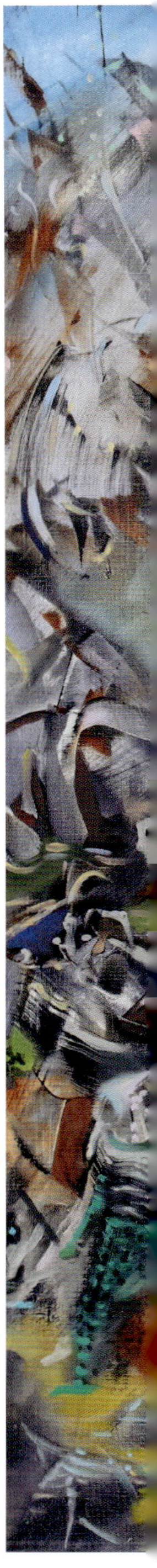

Hypocrisy of Democracy
2012
Oil on linen
76.2 x 91.4 cm
Private collection,
Brescia

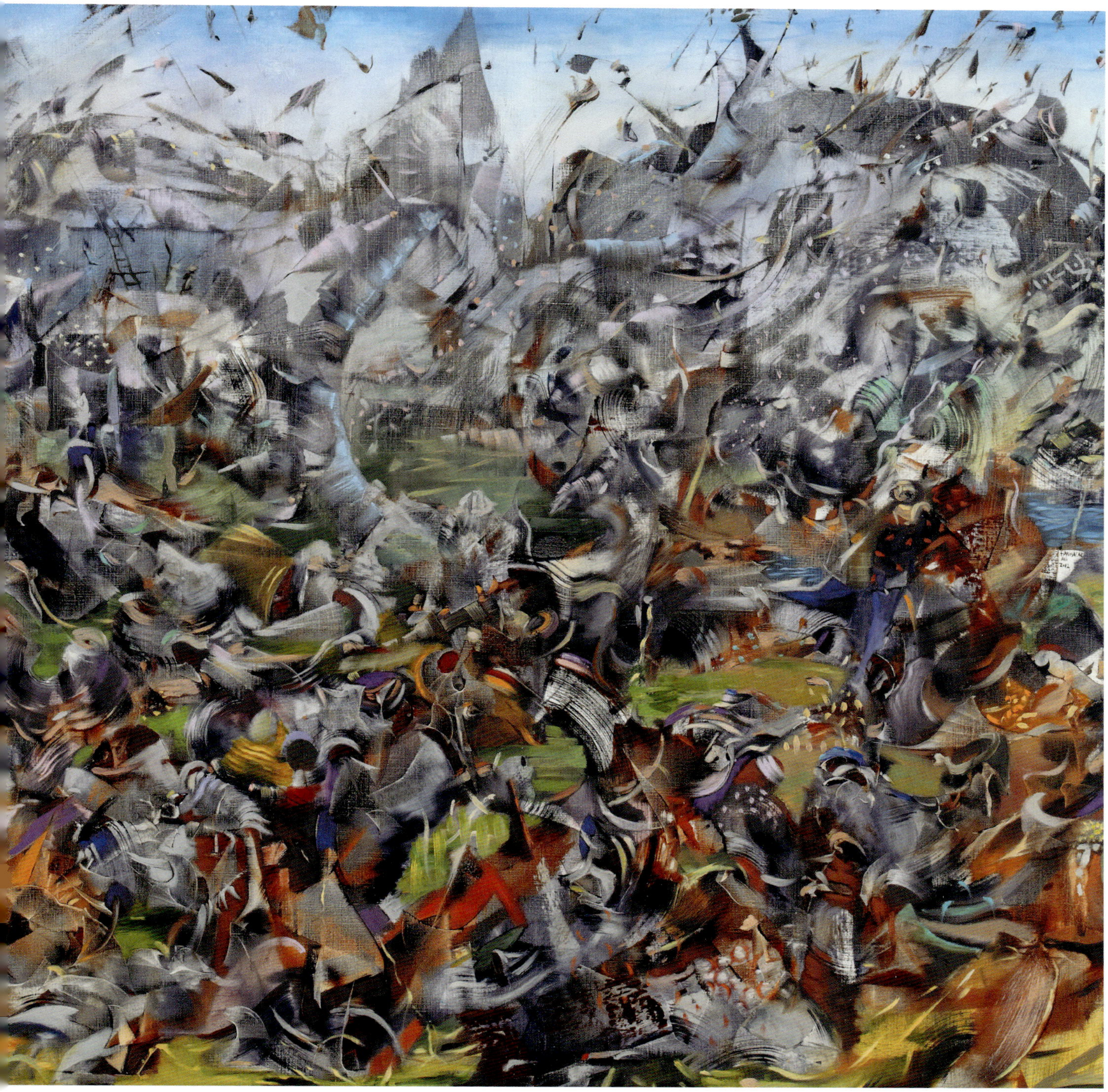

The Scream
2013
Oil on linen
61 x 61 cm
Private collection,
Milan

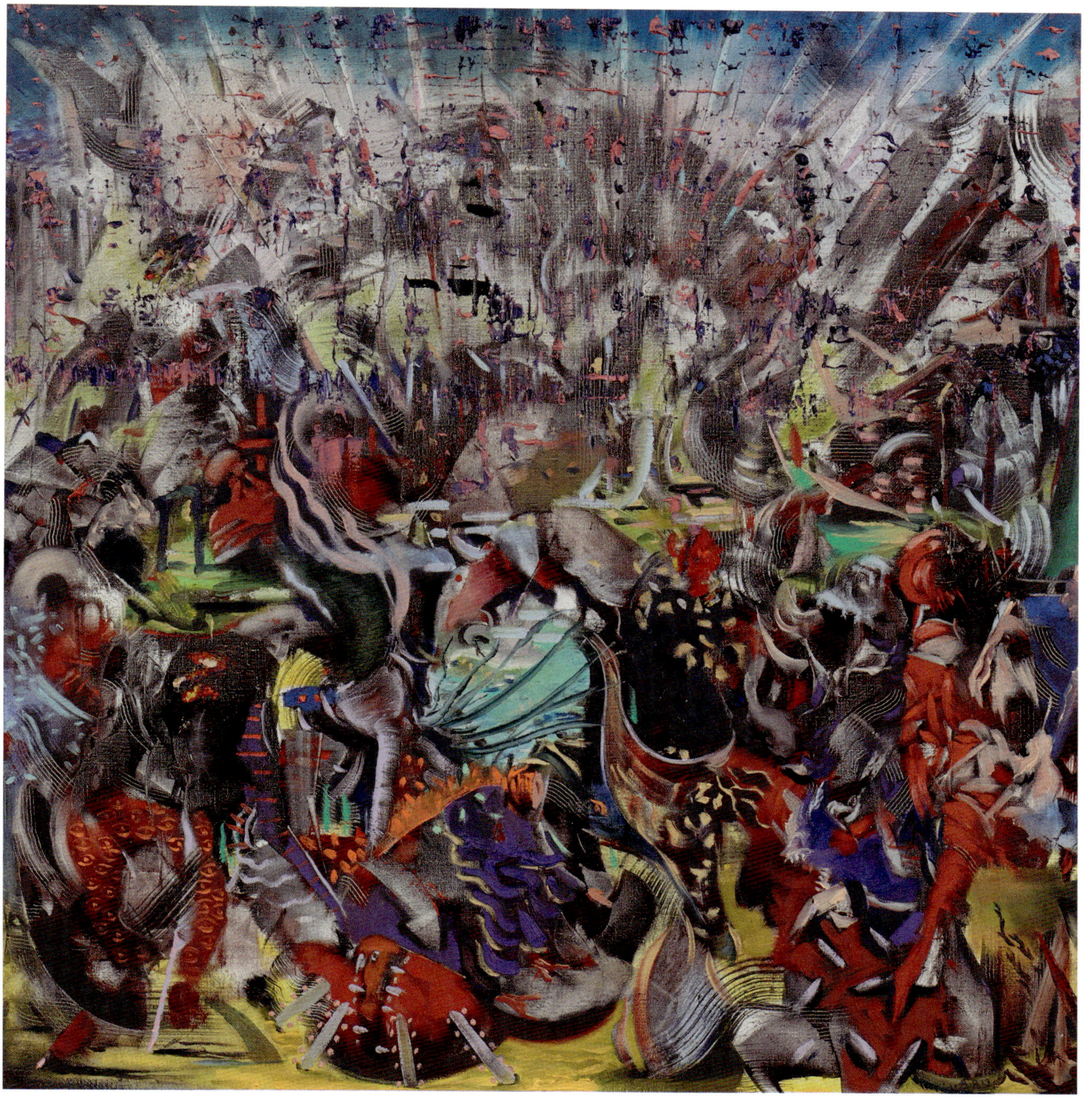

Melencolia I
2012
Oil on linen
91.4 x 76.2 cm
Private collection,
Salzburg

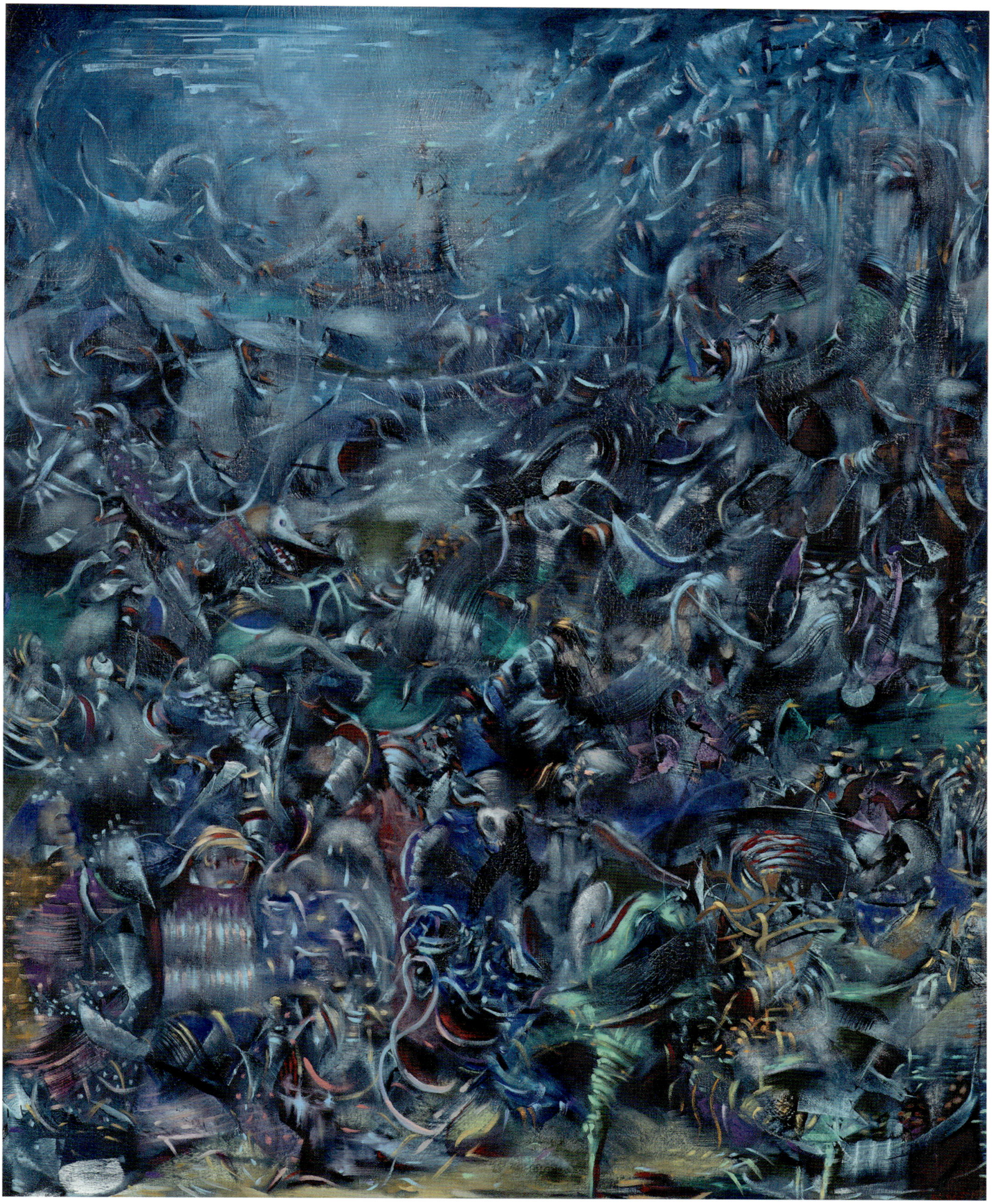

Carousel
2015
Oil on linen
61 x 61 cm
Private collection,
Milan

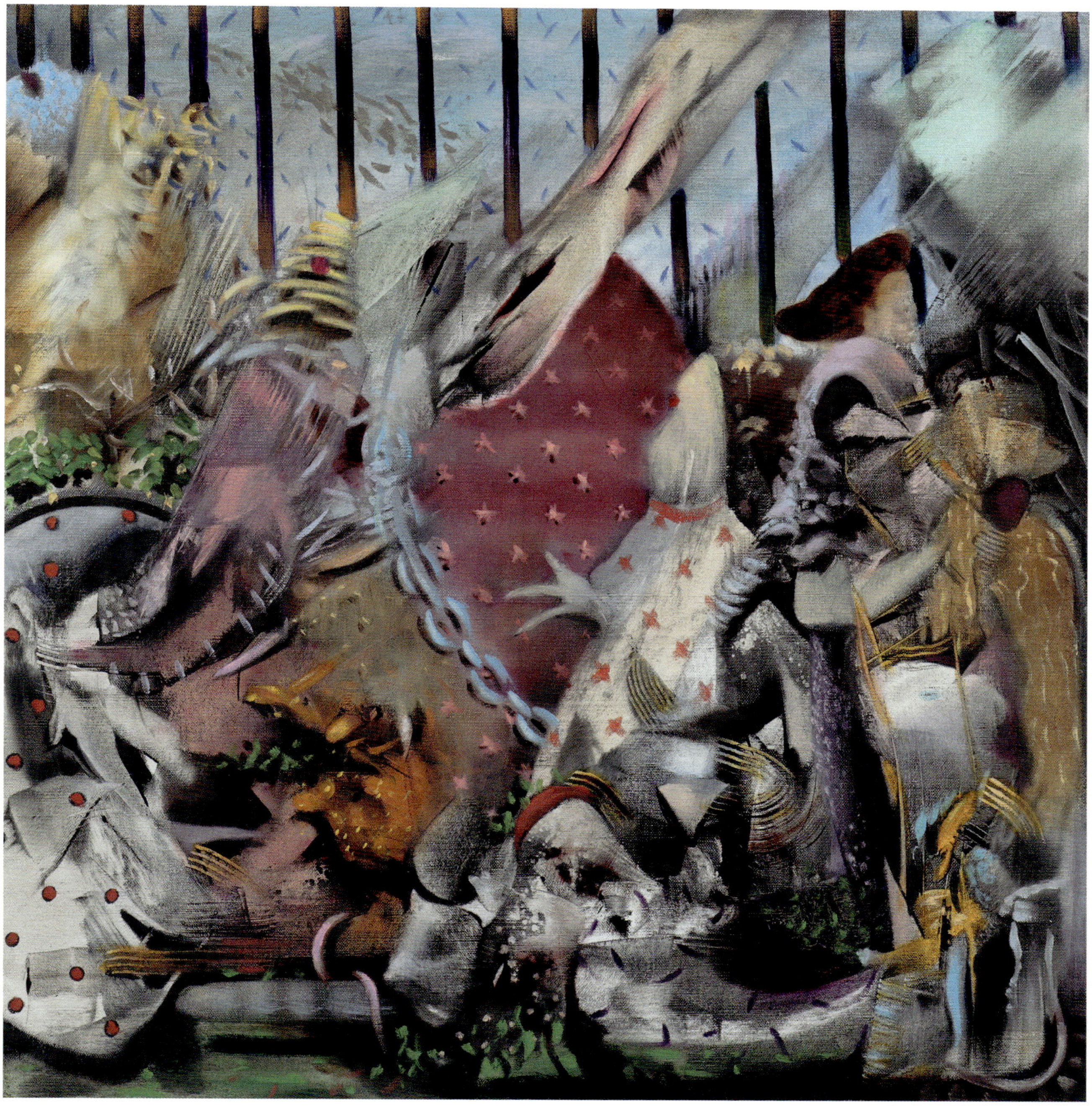

Ordered Disorders 1
2019
Oil on linen
40.6 x 50.8 cm
Private collection,
Milan

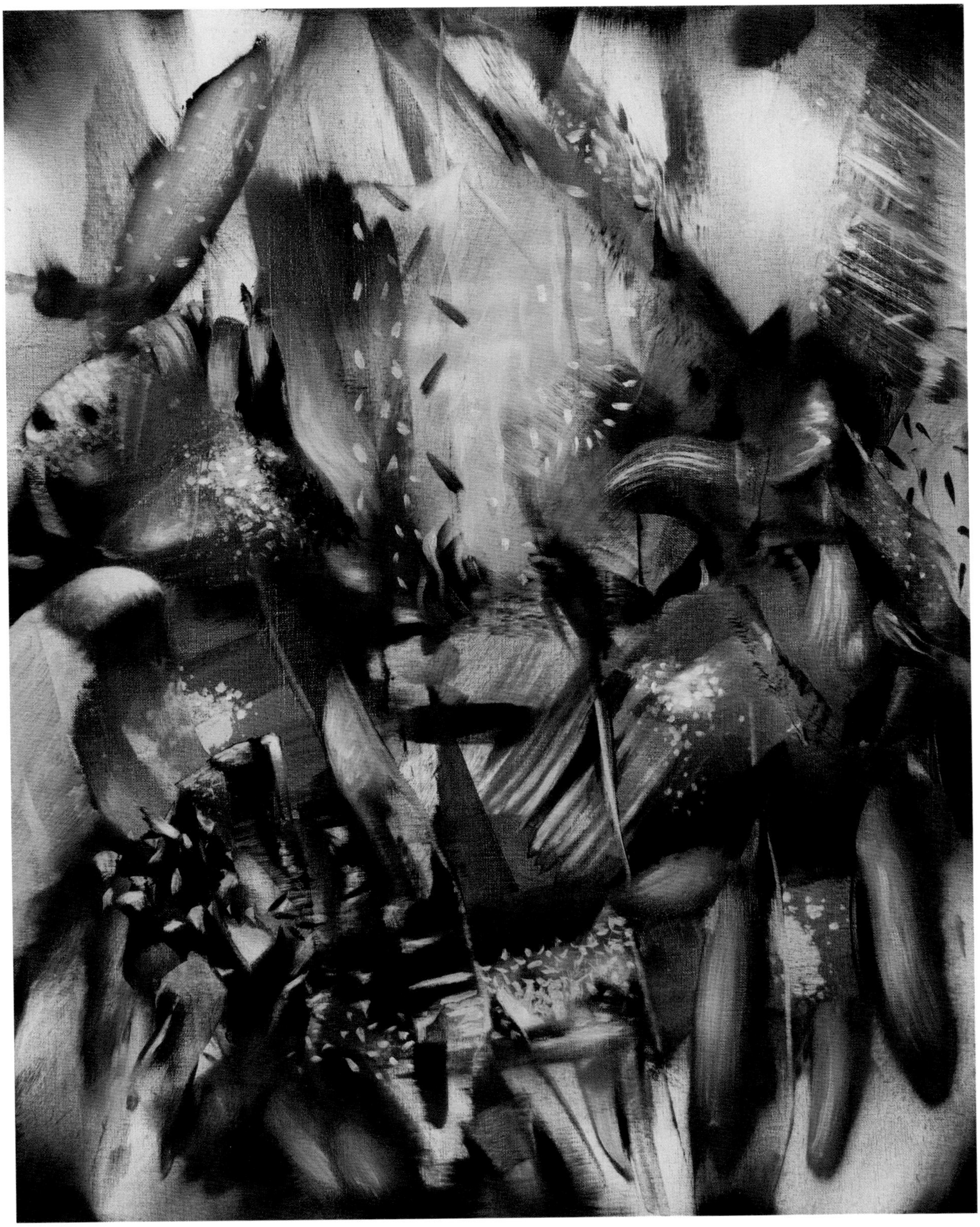

History
2012
Oil on linen
26 x 21 cm
Private collection,
Lyon

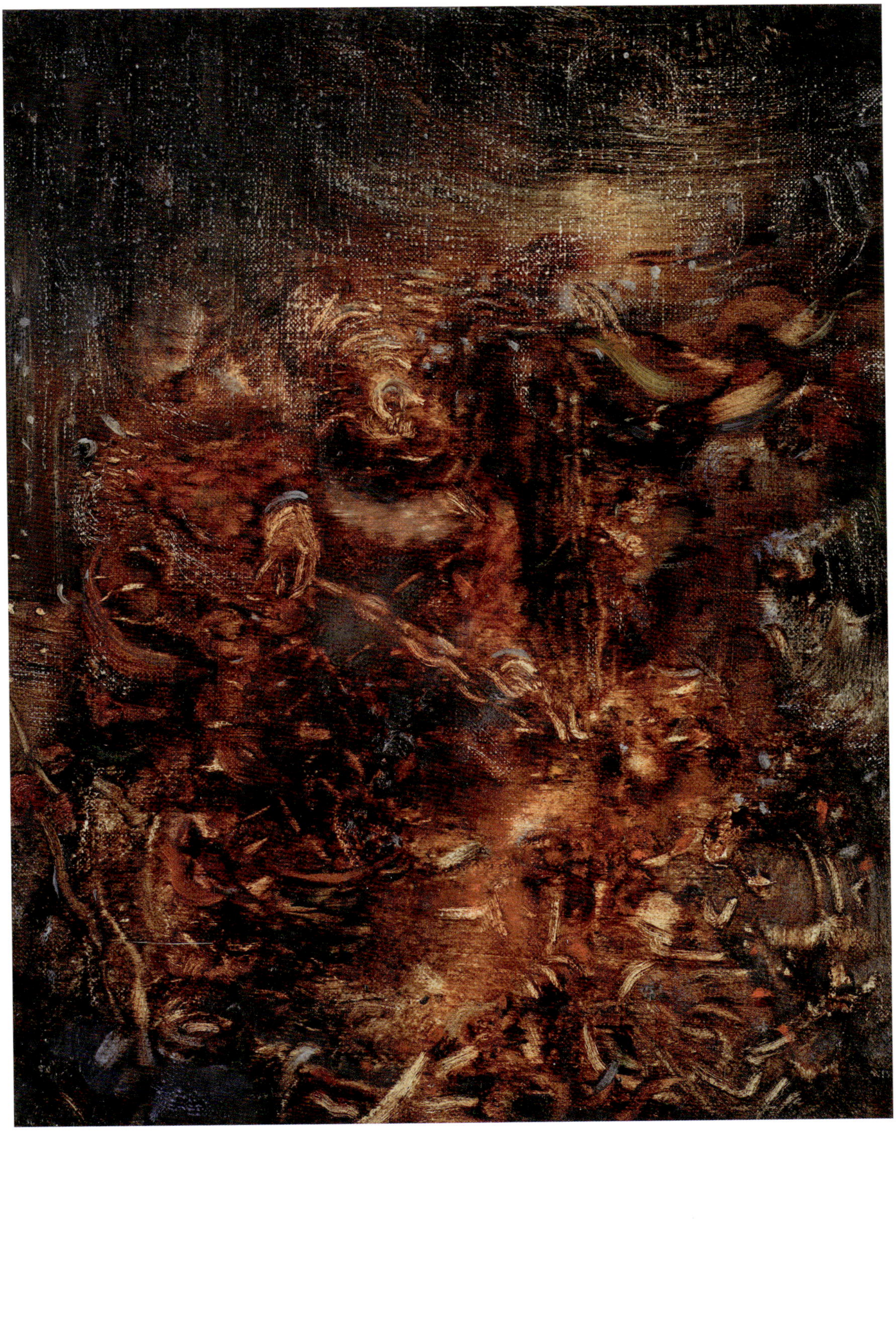

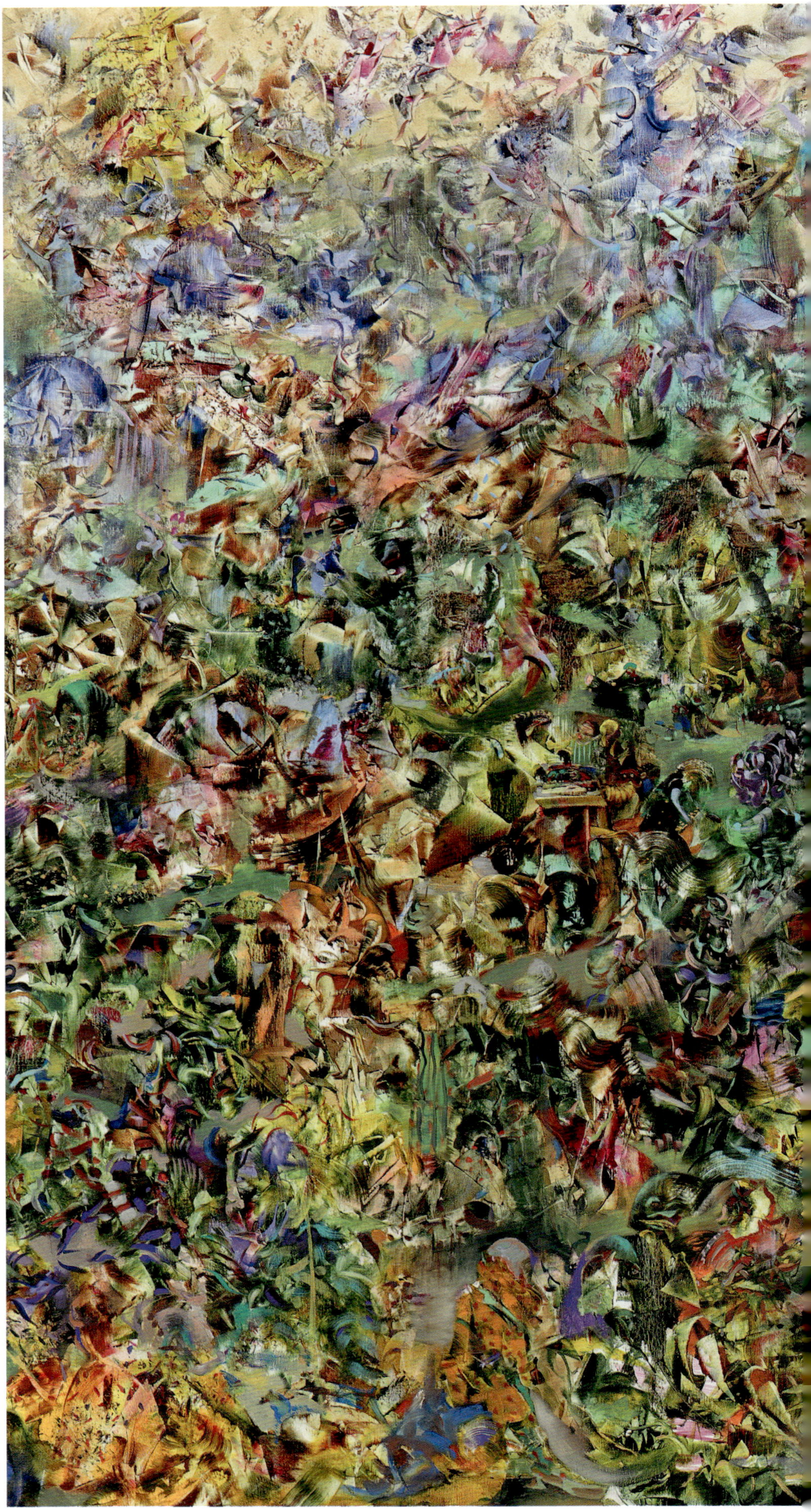

Selection
2011
Oil on linen
167.6 x 223.5 cm
Courtesy Thaddaeus Ropac, London, Paris, Salzburg

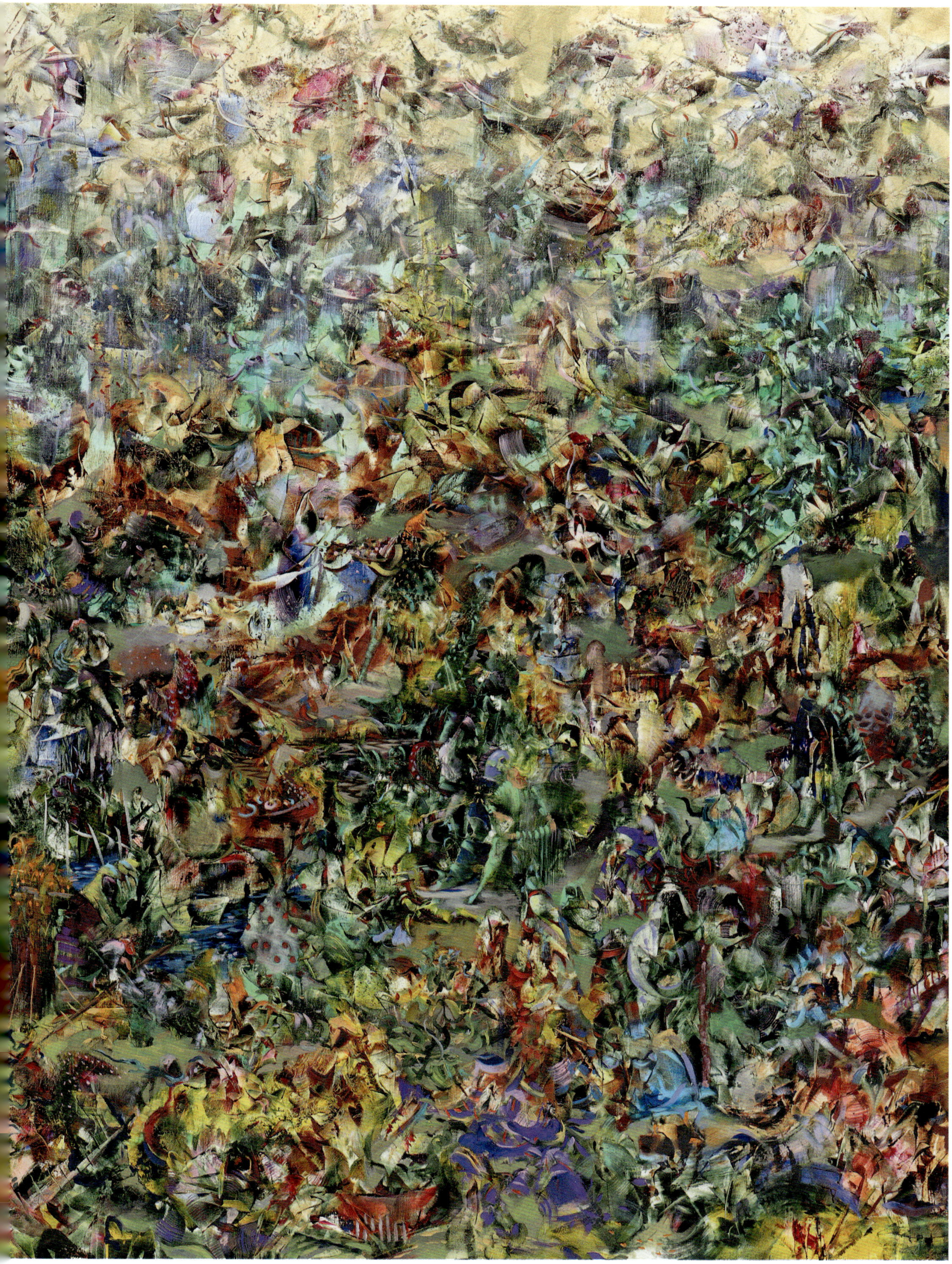

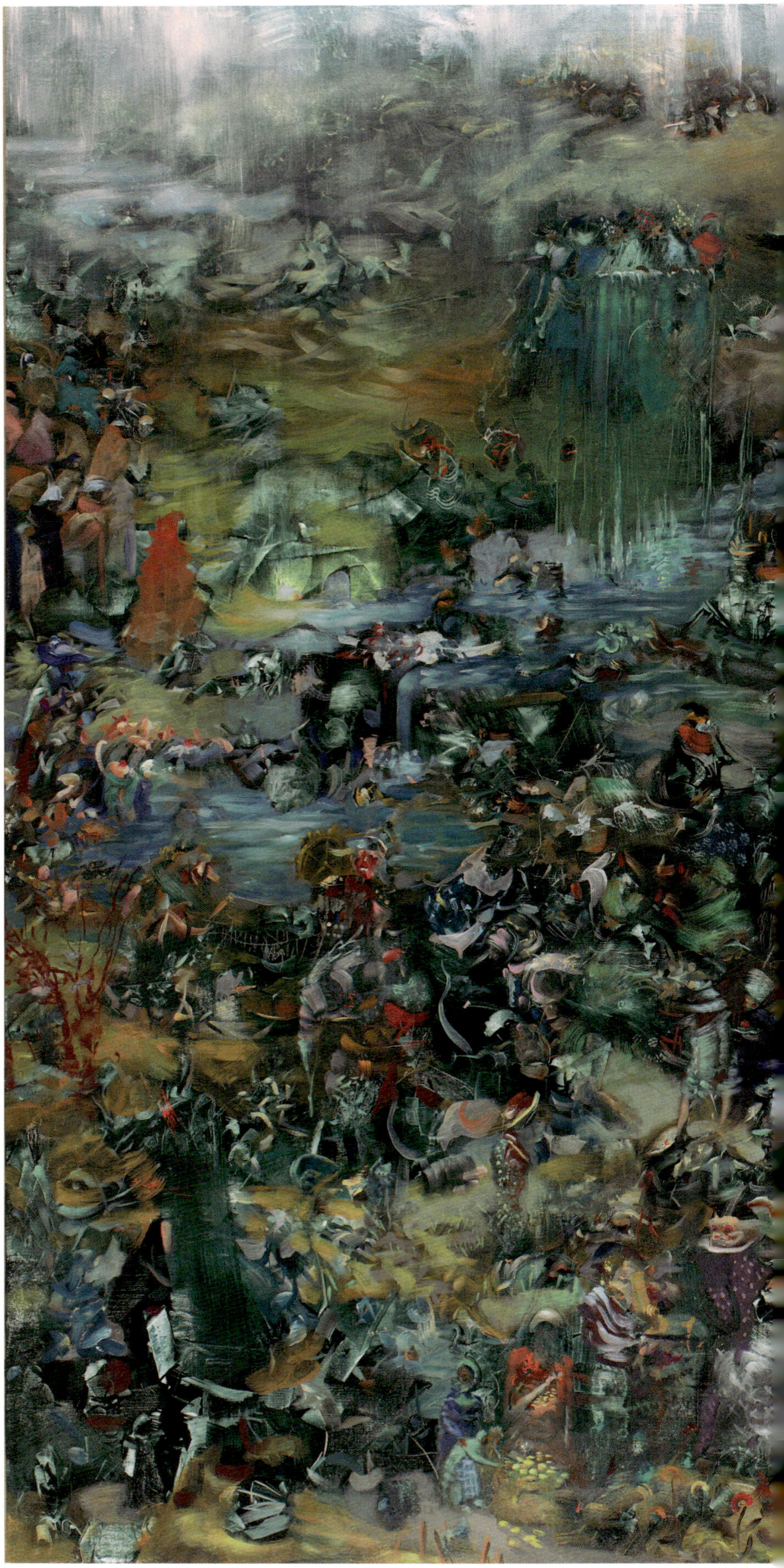

The Charlatans
2009
Oil on linen
137.2 x 182.9 cm
Courtesy Thaddaeus Ropac, London, Paris, Salzburg

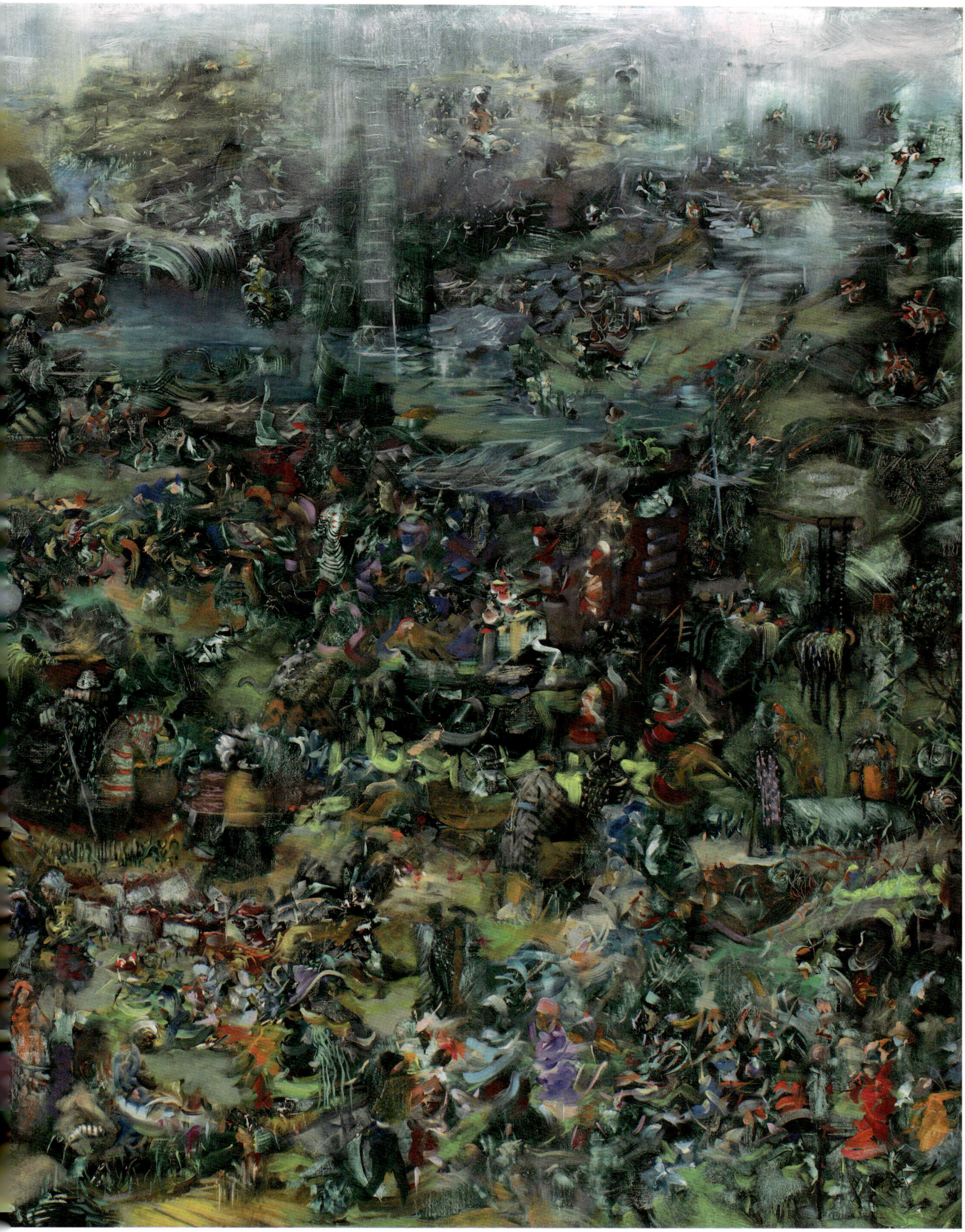

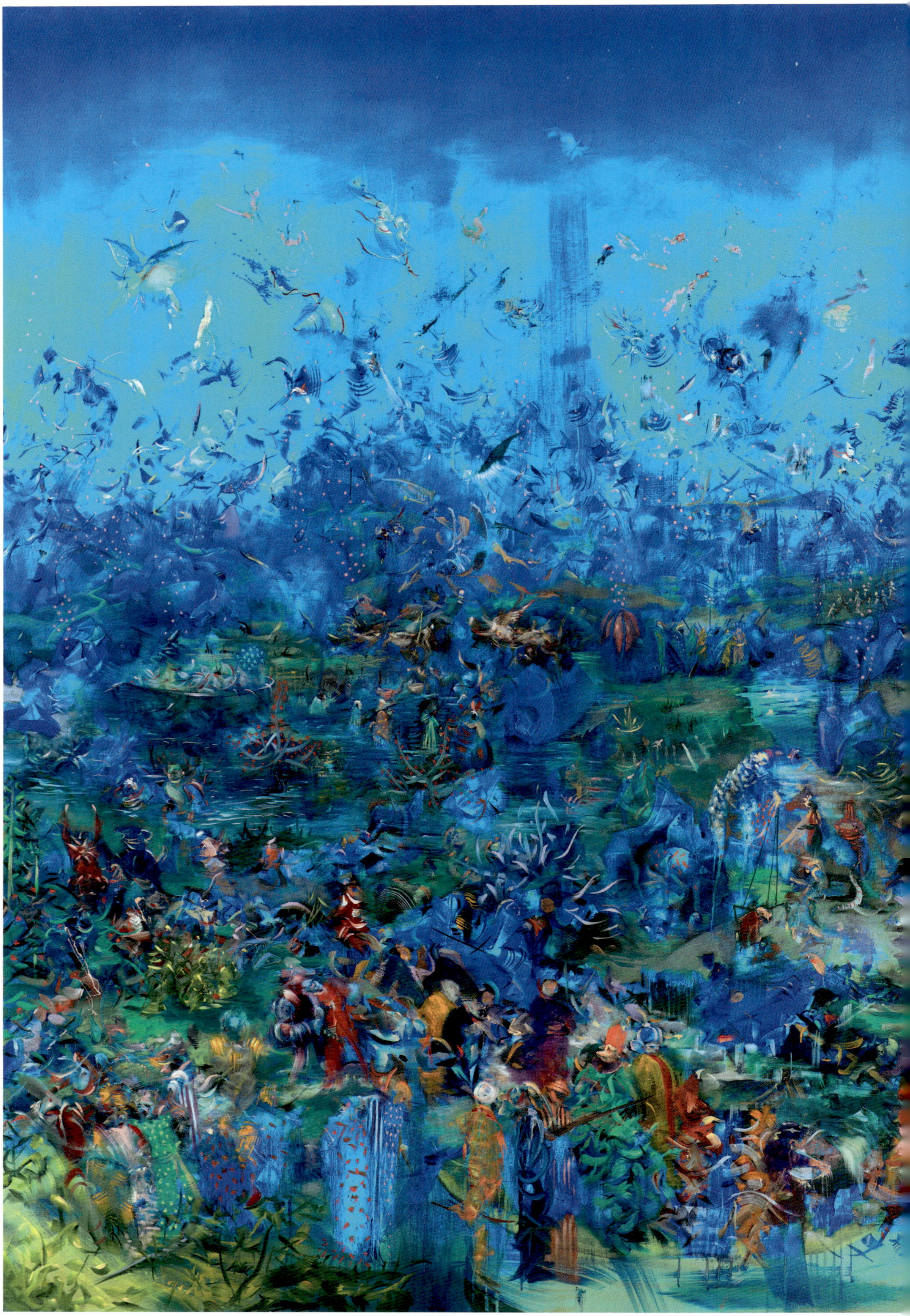

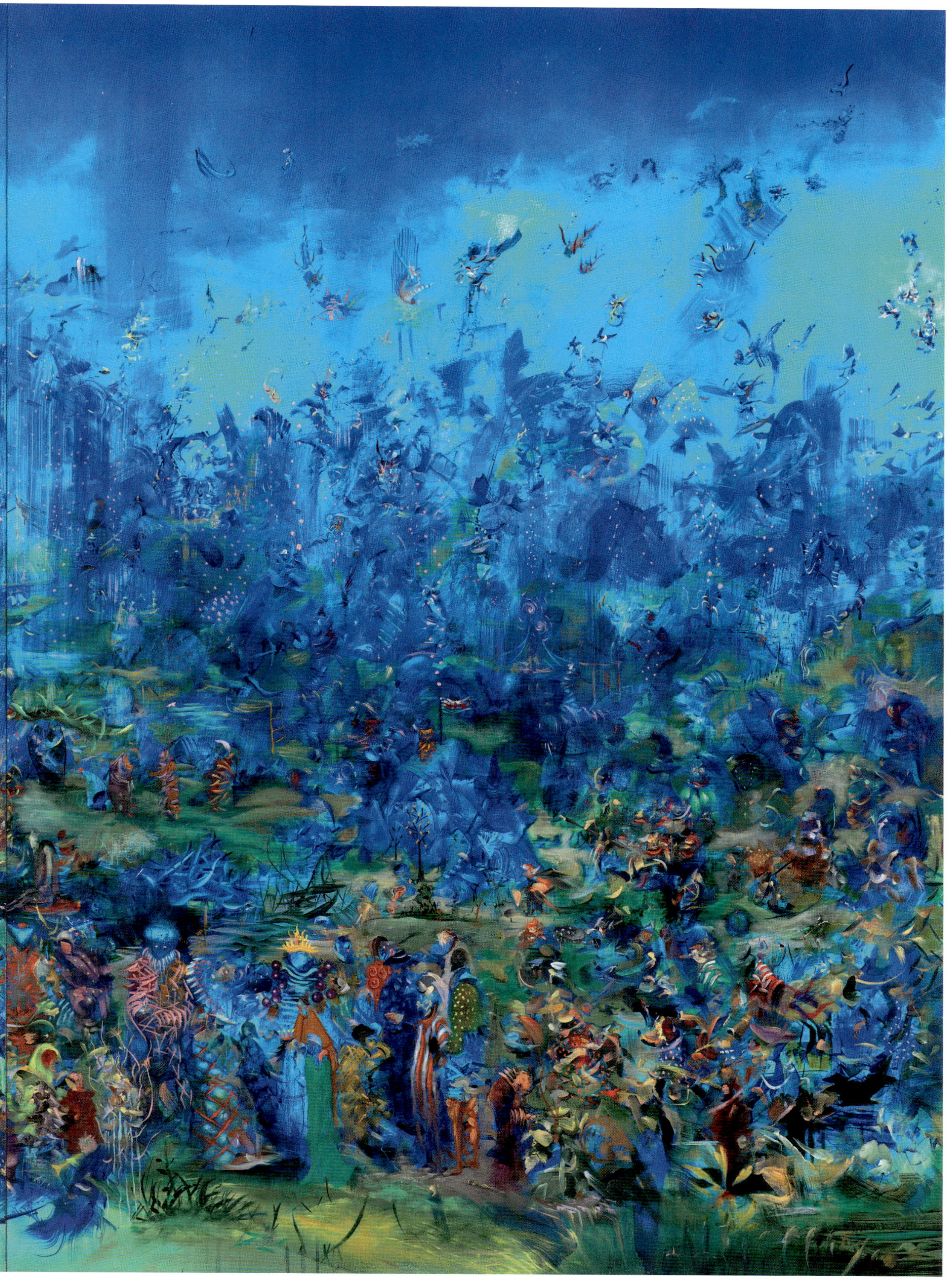

Pages 62-63:
The Gatekeepers
2009
Diptych, oil on linen
182.9 x 274.3 cm
(182.9 x 137 cm
each panel)
Courtesy Thaddaeus
Ropac, London,
Paris, Salzburg

What's Your Is Mine
2008
Oil on linen
61 x 45.7 cm
Private collection,
Milan

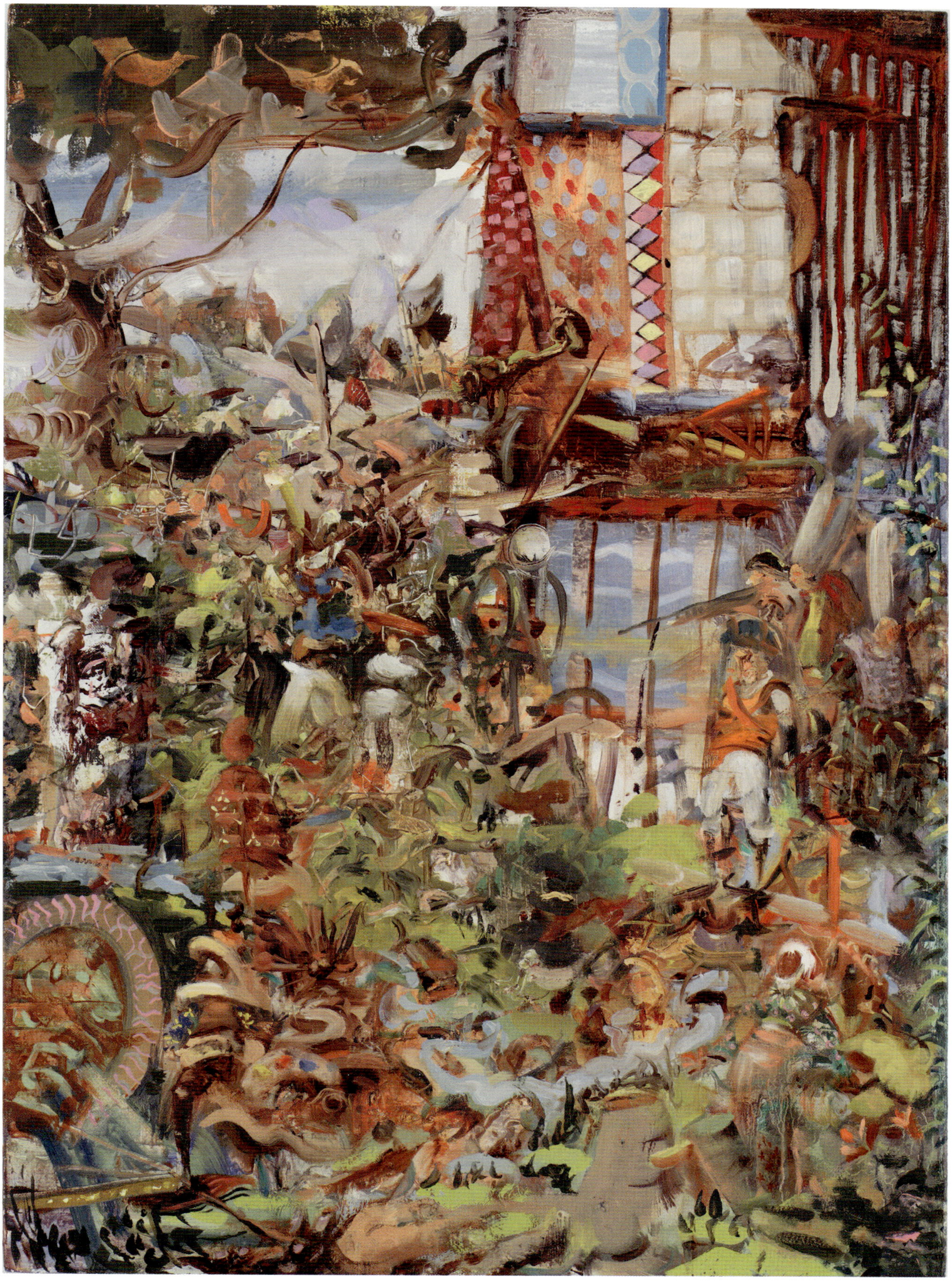

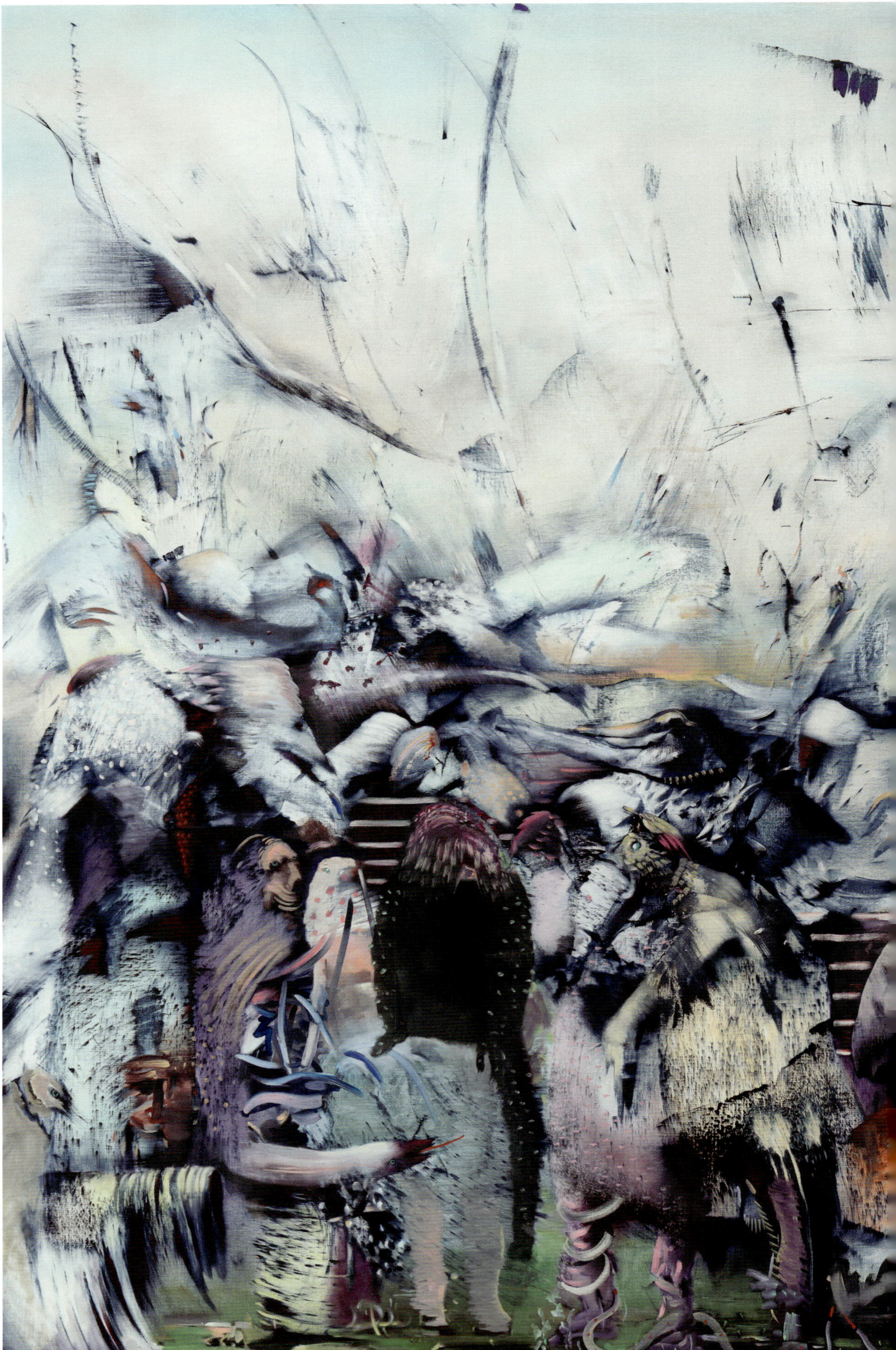

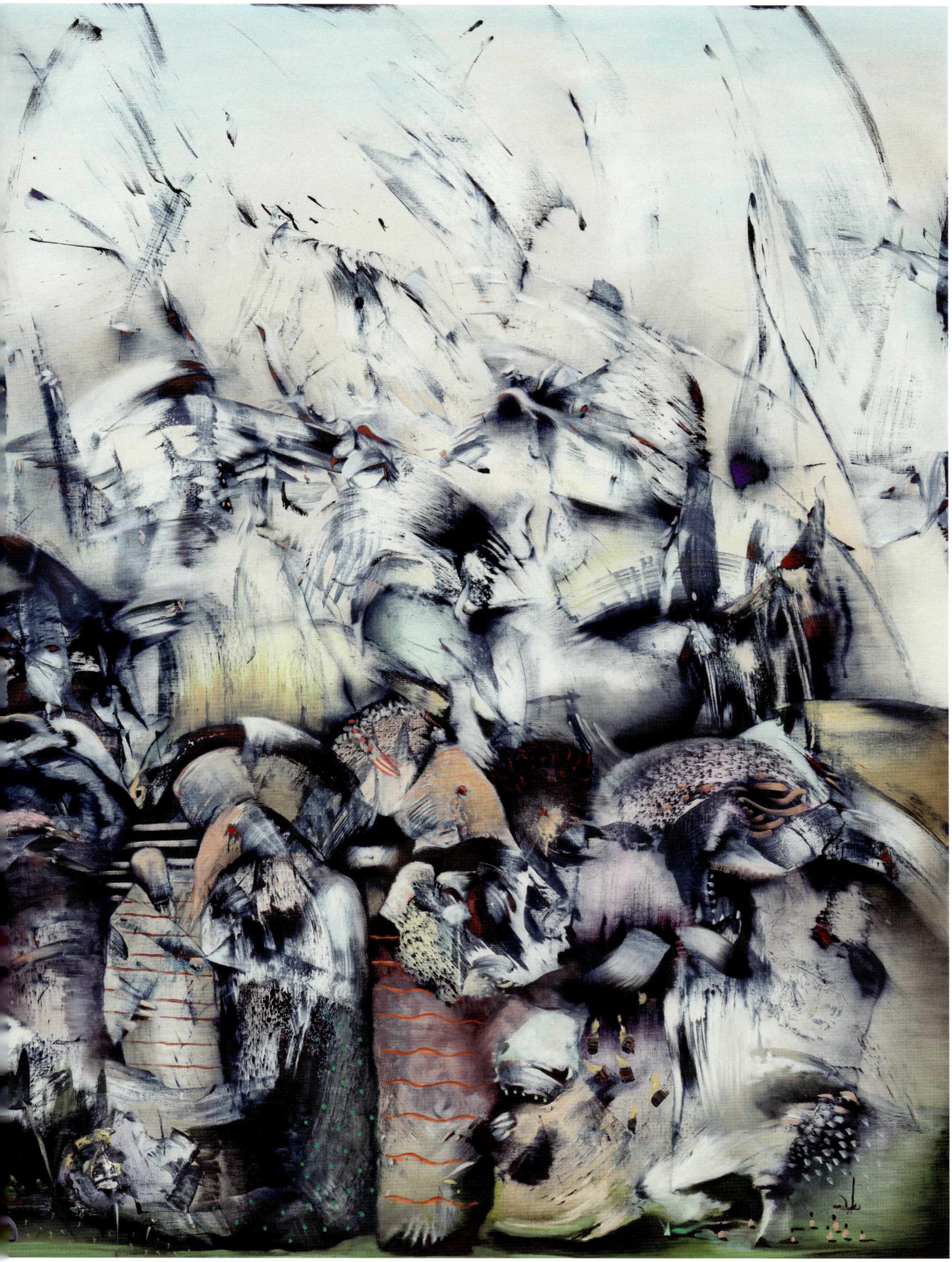

Pages 66-67:
Thought Police
2019
Oil on linen
208.3 x 304.8 cm
Private collection,
Hong Kong

Cannons Hidden in Roses
2019
Hand-coloured aquatint with photogravure, spitbite, drypoint and burnishing on Hahnemuhle copperplate
Bright White 300 gsm
Image
48.3 x 63.5 cm
Paper 68 x 80 cm
Ex. 23/25
Courtesy Thaddaeus Ropac, London, Paris, Salzburg

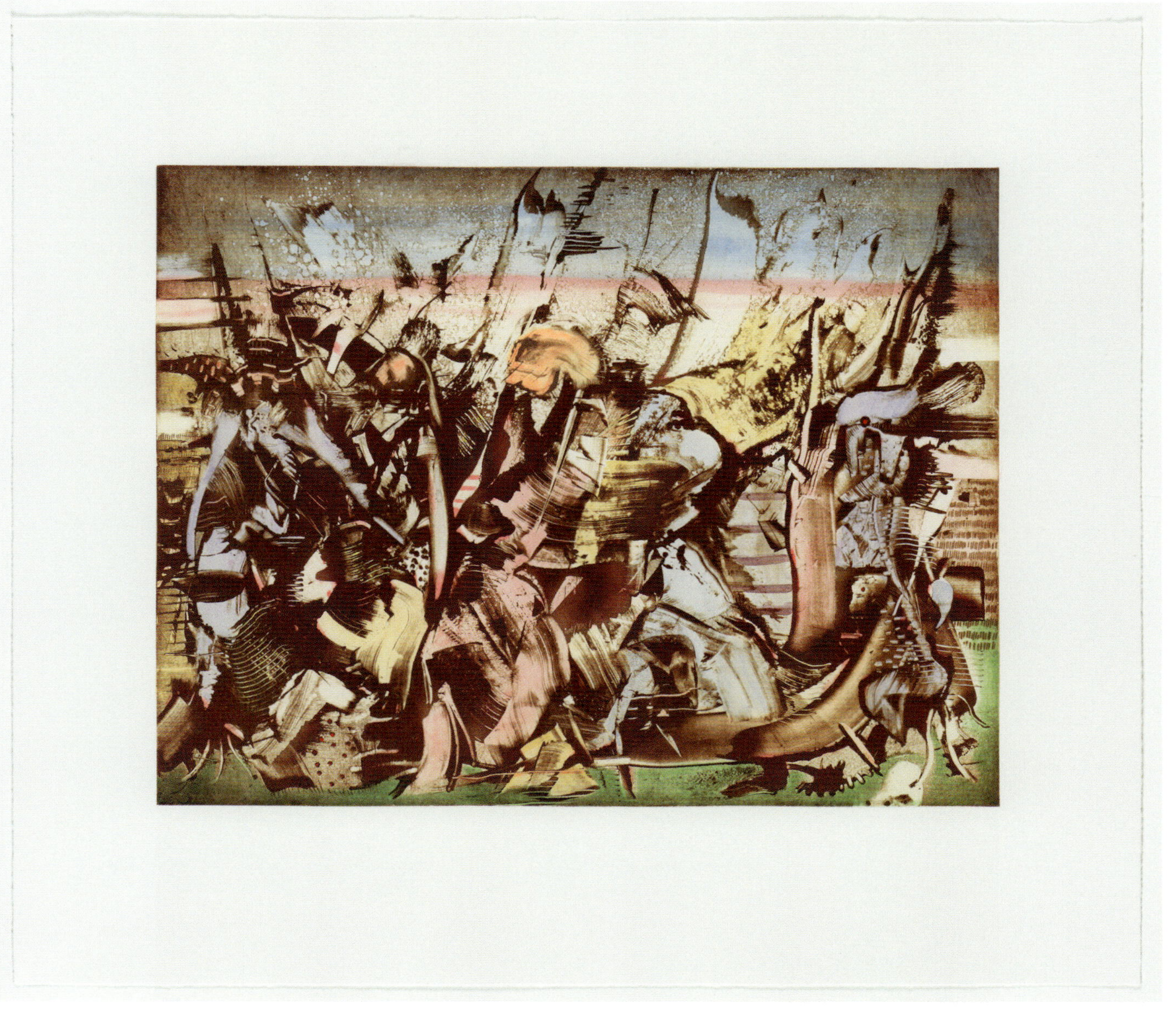

Nocturne
2019
Hand-coloured
aquatint with
photogravure,
spitbite, drypoint
and burnishing
on Hahnemuhle
copperplate
Bright White 300 gsm
Image
48.3 x 63.5 cm
Paper 68 x 80 cm
Ex. 23/25
Courtesy Thaddaeus
Ropac, London,
Paris, Salzburg

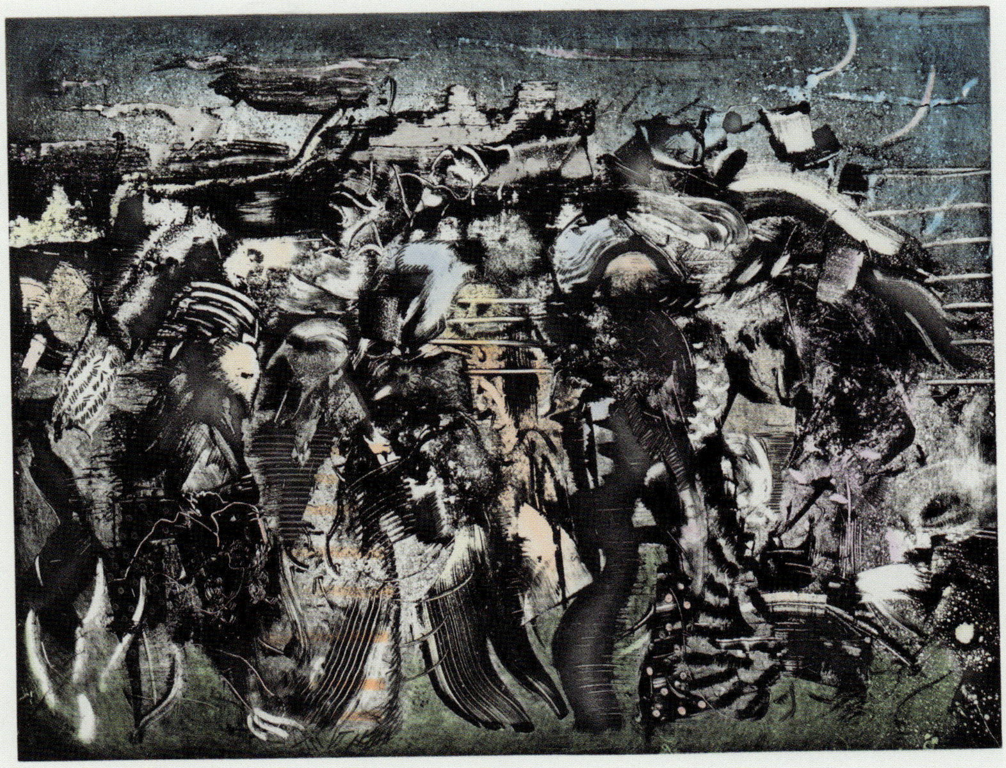

Blackwater
2010
Oil on panel
27.9 x 35.6 cm
Private collection,
Brescia

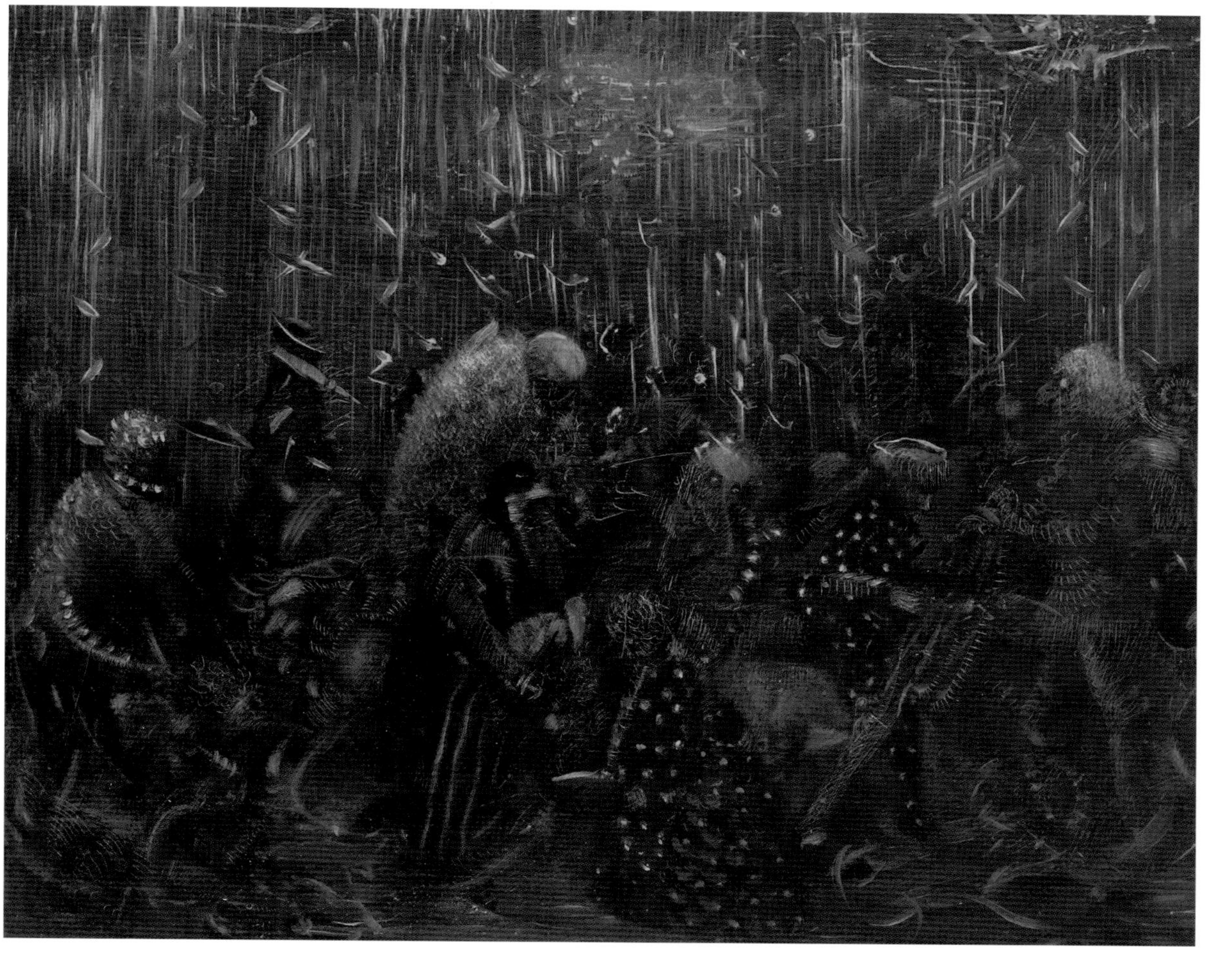

As Above
2009
Oil on linen
25.4 x 20.3 cm
Private collection,
Brescia

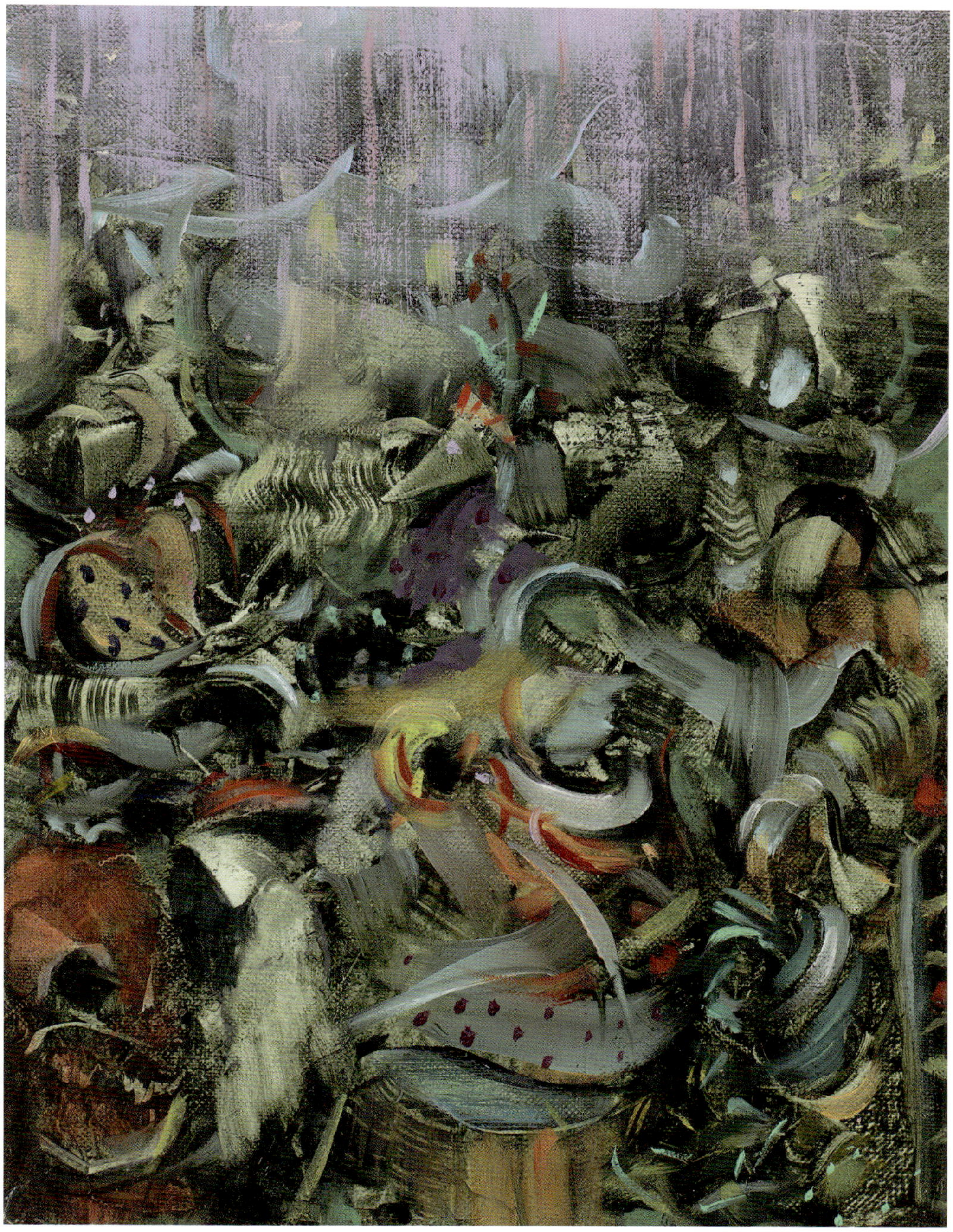

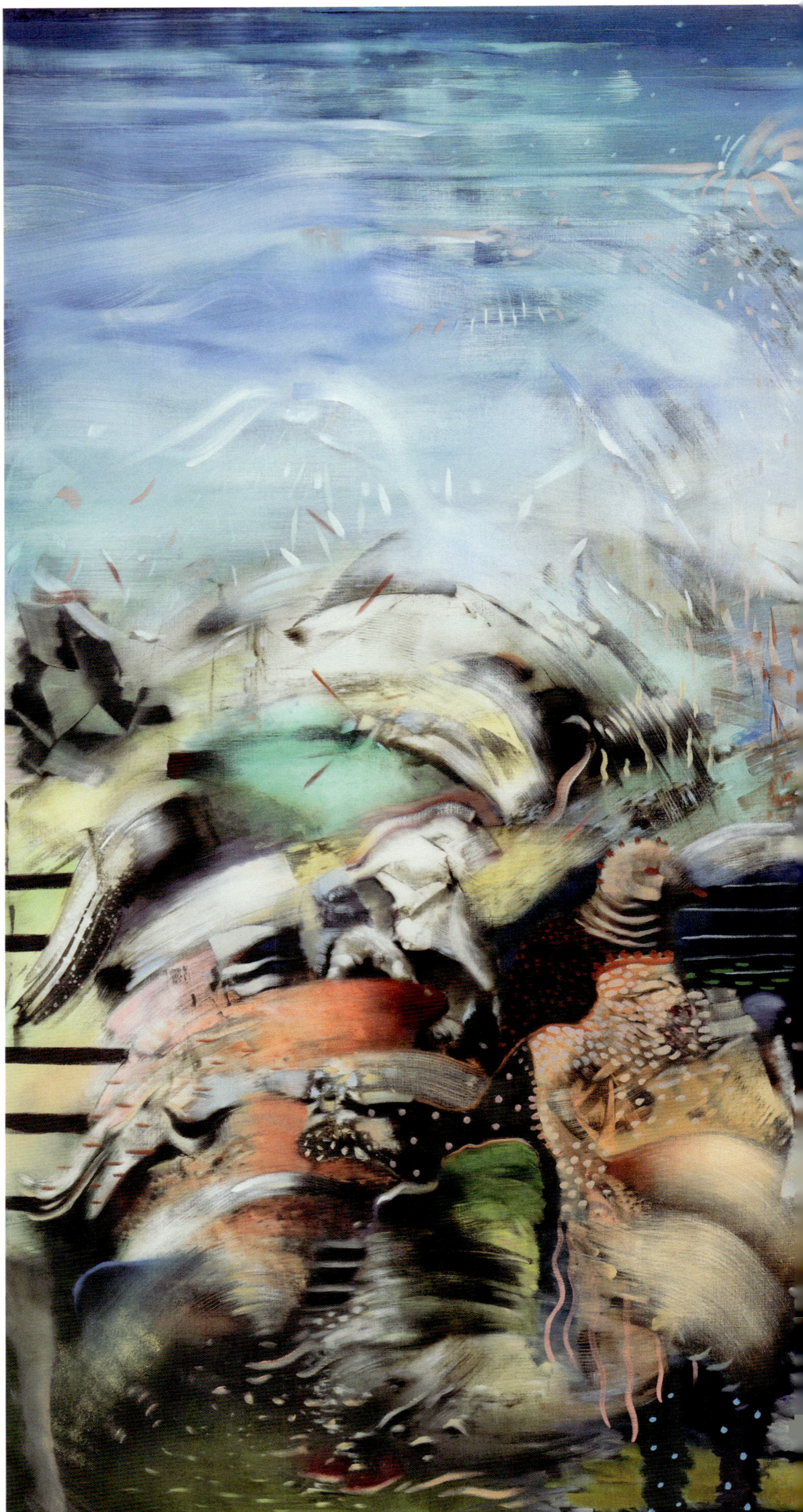

The Builder
2019
Oil on linen
167.6 x 223.5 cm
Private collection,
Berlin

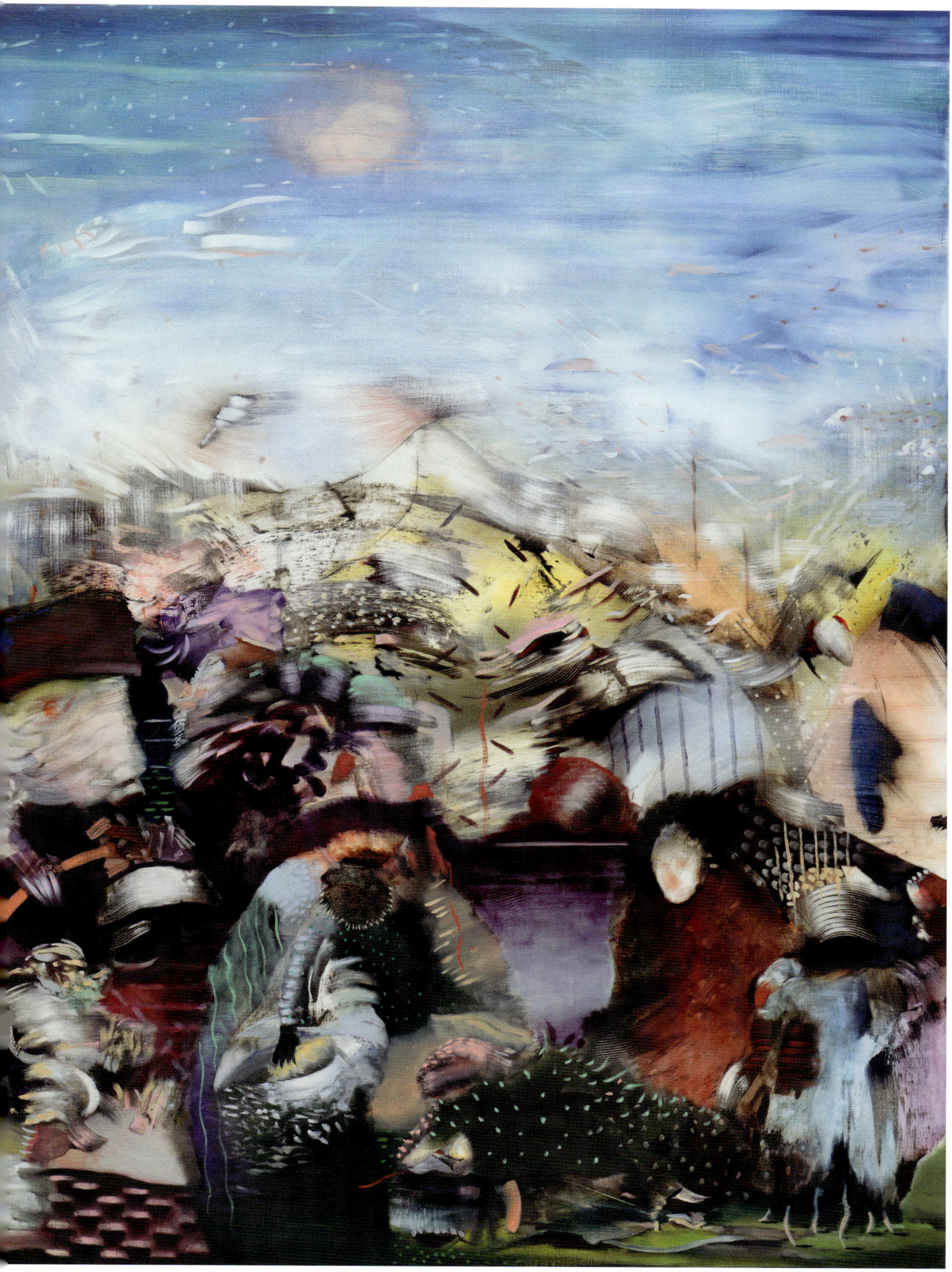

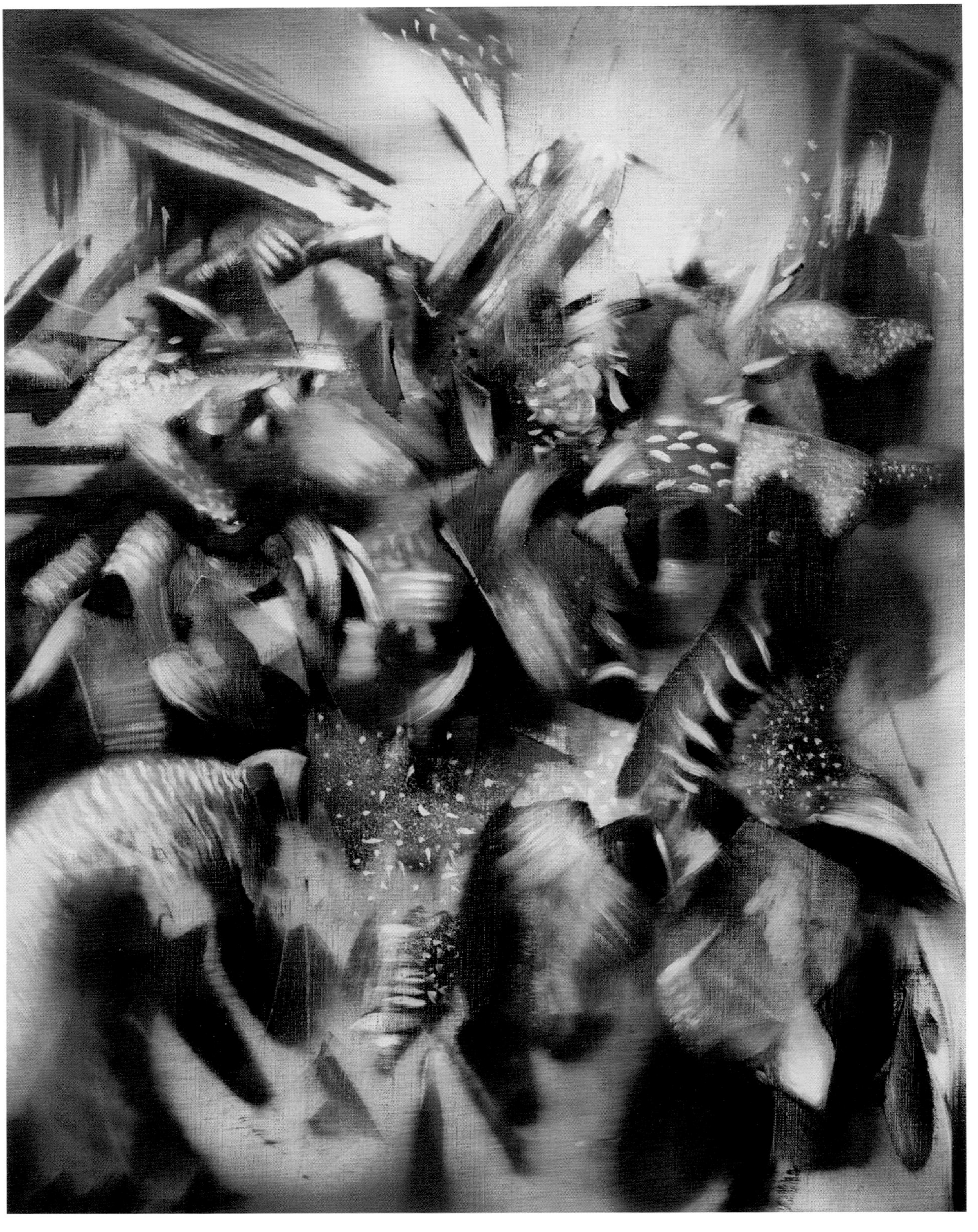

Ordered Disorders 2
2019
Oil on linen
40.6 x 50.8 cm
Private collection,
Paris

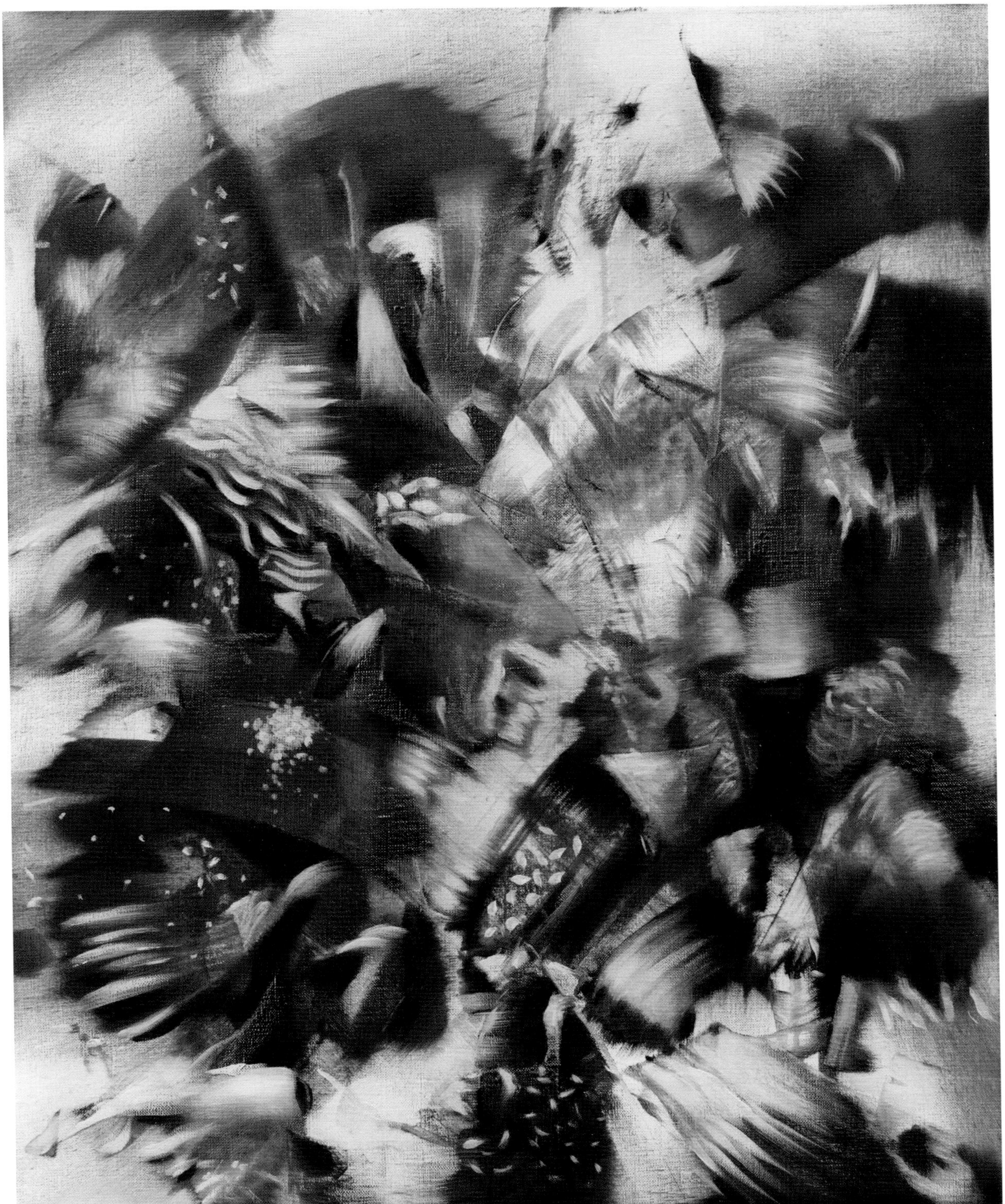

Ordered Disorders 4
2019
Oil on linen
40.6 x 50.8 cm
Private collection

I WOKE IN THE MIDDLE

Mary Jo Bang

It all makes perfect sense. We should feel threatened –
there where teeth, where claws,
where a body can act
as a weapon that can totally undo a human when-
ever the notable tendency for
gravity's law to stay
reliably steady is violently disregarded – leaving us
head over heels on our way
to a disaster-
ous instability. Uncertainty. Ambiguity. We know
the air at the top of the frame
is lighter than that
at the bottom. We know by seeing. We see and believe.
The bottom is occupied
by creatures that nightly
enter our sleep, in order to renew themselves. Ignore
us, we tell them, we're a part
of an adventure at the center
of an arboretum where trees stand in for breathing,
and an animal plays the role
of an actor enacting
this lesson: wearing a costume is somewhat the same
as looking at the world
below and over us.
A leg is not a lie. Nor is a wild boar. Nor is any "they"
who smugly say, "I am good,"
and "You are bad,"
but quite often get it wrong, forgetting what
an enormous achievement
being is. The red velvet shoe –
how does it do that trick of fitting a foot in while
also remaining suspended
in a mind where you
or I can find it whenever we wish to? Want to. Need to.
Of course, one has to know how
to enjoy what once was called
(Keats) negative capability: the more or less fathoming
of what one is content to
understand without
an "irritable reaching after fact and reason": "He
touched my hand as if
to tell me all
would be all right. / Then we crossed over from
where we'd been / into the inner
sanctum that houses hidden things."

Inferno, Canto III, lines 21-23. Dante Alighieri. [1265-
1321] Imagine watching
a parade of flora and fauna
sometimes dissolving, sometimes reconstituting itself
and coalescing into a mind
at work trying to conceive
how to say without saying: *I woke in the middle and had to*
find the way again; I needed
a guide and found one who
had taken similar risks in trying to embody the vastness of...
That is the problem,
the vastness – because
how can one erect a boundary around a world
so expansive, so multifarious.
Think: not only of atoms, but also
molecules, electrons, protons, Fibonacci sequences: 0,
1, 1, 2, 3, 5, 8, 13, 21, 34, 55,
89, 144, etcetera, etcetera.
The painter paints a movie of the mind and discovers
a way to stay inside
the lines by first
moving them, then wrapping them around a funnel
funneling everything
toward the center
of the earth where there, as Dante says, it's all ice and
embedded in the ice are those
who were, let's say,
"not nice" but instead chose to betray all aspects of
the social fabric that require
respect, a sense of evenness
& loyalty, to family, friends, & to that guest
in the vestibule, the one
you just invited in –
only to insert the classic dagger directly in its heart,
the blade a serpent's tongue, the wound
blushing like an arm
twisted and held behind your back, the capillary rush
of blood surfacing from under
crushed skin, the weight
of a leg as it bends forward, the knee grazed on tile,
gravel, concrete or asphalt,
the breath knocked
from the lungs. It's here where you learn to see –
"The inferno of the living is not
something that will be;

if there is one, it is what is already here, the inferno
where we live every day,
that we form by being together" –
Italo Calvino, *The Invisible Cities*. Which is another
way of saying Hell is,
as Sartre says, *les autres*.
And as Dante has Virgil say, You must see it in order
to believe it. And now imagine
watching every step
you make while moving circle to circle always getting
nearer to some heavenly rescue –
unlike here on earth
where not even reason can help you see through
the haze of where you've been
and where you are going,
as well as where you want to be. Where is that? Who
can say since you can
only see what is
in front of you. Imagine a sea filled with the unseen.
A Hell inhabited by those
you know and those
you don't from every era but now, they have taken
new forms: just so, the porcupine
will still have its
sharp barbs covering everything but its abdomen and
will still know
how to use them and
will still adamantly refuse to give them up no matter
that a promise of better
hangs in the balance.
"Better," it asks, what's that? When you see it, you will
see the extraordinary assembled
along the sight line,
each carrying with it some semblance of wholeness but
only a hint of what it could be.
It could be
a new Garden of Earthly Delights mixed with a school
of fish, frogs, or a plague
named after the same. It's fine
that we don't know. Anything we do know will see us
through the repeating days
and nights that are
a life. You can see how an allegory can become a path
by which we perceive
the invisible play-within-a-play.

Blue gingham can be worn by a girl back in Kansas
while in Italy, the Tuscan poet
gets up each day
and puts on his long red robe. We all agree, that world
is more complicated
than the other. The key
to each is that here, as there, and everywhere, monsters
signify our own shortcomings:
like Dante's diviners
who can see everything in the future but know nothing
about the present.
In "Love & Death,"
Byron says (more or less) I watched the storm. Watched
the fever watching from a grave.
The earthquake, the quivering
wall, the faintest thought, the gasp of death. And love.
The parade you see
at the bottom of the canvas
called *Beautiful Lies* contains the poet, riding a lion
or some other beast,
wearing a crimson coat
and polka-dot pants, why not? Blake makes both Dante
and Virgil androgynous
in long diaphanous dresses,
the better to see the duality in each of us: Jung's anima/
animus, Freud's "polymorphic
perverse disposition"
"which every nursemaid knows" (Jones, 350). To be
obvious is to take the complicated
and turn it
into a simple conclusion, which can best be done in
cartoons, greeting cards
and board games
but not in art. Art is the beautiful lie. In art, I am not I
but some supposed person
on an invented path which
always begins I woke in the middle of what we call our
life and found my way
to a canvas covered with muchness.

The Scream
Museo
Stefano Bardini

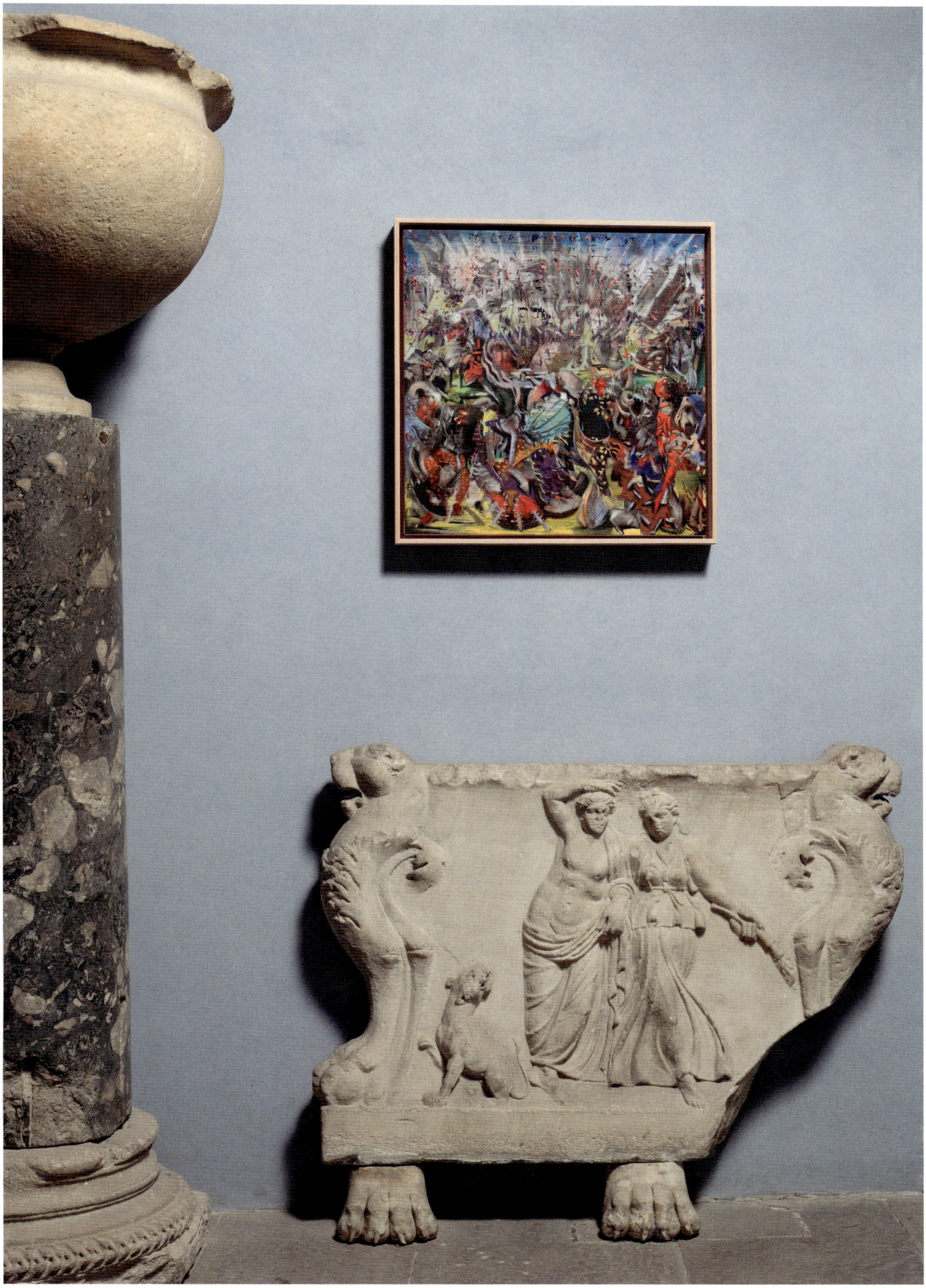

HELL ACCORDING TO ALI, BETWEEN TINTORETTO AND JUNG

Chiara Gatti

"It's all in the *Inferno*", affirms Ali Banisadr, reiterating it several times with Olympian calm: "Hell says it all". He moves his hands as he talks, before thrusting them into his jeans and glancing out of the lead window into the light of the Piazza della Signoria. Inside the Sala delle Udienze of the Palazzo Vecchio in Florence his warm voice booms a little beneath the coffered ceiling and the frescoes of the Gauls being driven out of Rome. "I feel overawed by these noble spaces; to think that Cosimo de' Medici once sat on that throne [...]" he says, pointing to the high-backed wooden chair behind an austere desk. The large door leading to the Sala dei Gigli portrays Dante and Petrarch, facing each other on the two inlaid wings of the doors. "Two giants. But I feel at home with Dante now". In preparation for the Florence exhibition, he studied the *Divine Comedy* with the painstaking diligence of a philologist, searching for shades of meaning to translate into painting, into site-specific paintings to showcase here during celebrations to mark the 700th anniversary of the poet's death. And which, with every gesture of the spatula, sink towards the centre of the earth, into the entrails of a castigated humanity, amid murmurs and cries rendered in shades of colour at once dark and psychedelic.

Have you really read the whole of the *Divine Comedy*?

No, I must confess, just the *Inferno*, but in four different editions. My favourites are the ones translated by Robert Hollander and by Mary Jo Bang, an American poetess and Dante scholar. I believe there are over sixty modern translations of Dante in English. I looked for the incisive ones, which I hoped would render in as granular a way as possible the nuances of the original language – the most precise language to convey a specific message, which I needed or wanted to express in painting.

Did you succeed?

Dante used to say that all his work sprang from the truth. That every message concealed in the *Divine Comedy* was the fruit of a reflection on reality; it stemmed from a fact, situation or even just a detail. I've read and reread the *Inferno* as the product of this examination of life and as a reflection of life itself. The *Inferno* is encyclopaedic in this respect. It contains and absorbs every kind of knowledge. It's the reservoir of a universal and totalizing knowledge running through human history to the present age. And which still speaks about us today: about exile, violence and greed, but hope too. Without inventing anything. Without imagining anything. It's all true. As painting should be.

And isn't it?

Painting, by its very nature, can appear to be a lie, because it is just the representation of the real. But sometimes a line of poetry or the image of a painting make us cry. It's in that moment that you realize how real they are. Because they hit home. That's why I studied the *Inferno*, for its inexorable truth.

So you've explored the current relevance of Dante?

I immersed myself in him, in his words, in his episodes. And the more I got into him, the more I plunged into eternal themes. I think Dante wrote in the vernacular to get through to people, to be contemporary and pedagogical. To embrace the lesson of his work, I added part of my own personal history, of our actuality and an artistic idiom suited to the present day. I looked at the works of artists who have interpreted the *Divine Comedy*, from William Blake to Robert Rauschenberg and his prints, with their wealth of references to political figures of his time and to American society after the Second World War. The *Divine Comedy* is so immortal that it can speak to every age and geographic location. Like Hieronymus Bosch's *Last Judgement* triptych in Vienna, which I saw as a child. They are works that grab you. You stand in front of them rooted to the spot, and you can't drag yourself away, because they are like mirrors of your soul.

Which canto do you prefer most?

The XXVIII, in the Malebolge, where Dante and Virgil meet Mohammad. We are almost in the deepest part of the afterlife, where the setting becomes cruel and iniquitous. Relying on pure poetry, Dante evokes the great conflicts of the past, the wars waged by the Romans, all those who died in the Second Punic War, the invasion of the Normans, then the Angevins and the Swabians, in order to compare them with the wounds and mutilations at the bottom of the *bolgia* and to introduce the encounter with the prophet of Islam. There's no single truth here. I am struck by how Dante manages to make different stories converge in a single place. It's as if every war is like every other. It's not about a single conflict, but about violence in general. It's an absolute discourse.

Multiplicity converges into a single story in your paintings as well.

I move from Egypt to Mesopotamia, from Persian miniatures to Japanese prints and through to the contemporary. In a single flow, but one that is never linear; it is a spiral, like the double helix of DNA. Without limits. I might also suggest a view, an episode, a figure, but they are just pretexts to touch on universal themes: exodus, death, abuse, pain and the origin of pain itself. Descending into the heart of the earth is a kind of therapy for Dante, a psychoanalytic investigation. The abyss is a metaphor of the unconscious, a buried root of the Jungian collective consciousness. A journey to the centre of the soul.

Littered with battles, in your case...

Because these are metaphors too. Like Tintoretto's *Battles*: the mythological dimensions of his pictures exalt the triumph but carry a premonition of the fall. This master's sensitive painting has a symbolic value that addresses the inexorable flow of time, the perception of finiteness contained in his vibrant and high-strung universe. I try to follow the same emotional rhythm in my painting, where everything emerges and then sinks away. Everything vanishes. I learnt this from Velázquez and his visual deceptions. The eye completes the lacunae in the image. The brain fills in the holes of vision. Not like the Flemish artists, who, with their lucidity, always revealed everything in an almost didactic way. I strive for a painting that insinuates and alludes, without descending into narrative. That evokes, without losing the mystery. That is not rational but activates our visual mind.

Painting as a passageway to the elsewhere?

I like to think of painting as a threshold. A door into the invisible. Painting has a powerful spiritual dimension. A mystical power projecting into the sphere of the intangible. Ultimately, in the history of ancient painting, viewers – worshippers – saw painting as a passage. As in the case of Byzantine icons. A way between the visible and the invisible. And now, between the past and present. We can see it in all those massive themes that have traversed the centuries and which still concern us today. Migration, abuse, war.

Of which you have first-hand experience.

I fled from the Iranian Revolution and from the Iran-Iraq war. I grew up in wartime. I witnessed the tragic manifestation of the dark side of humanity. I saw what human beings are capable of doing to each other. As a child I transformed them into monsters that kill. Dante said that no one is good or evil. In his own way, he created hybrids in his world. Beings that descended as beasts and came back up as angels. But there is a bestial side to all of us, and, unfortunately, I have experienced it directly. Hence some of my combinations between human being and beast, animal and plant, machine and individual. Like in the anamorphoses of Hieronymous Bosch. Every time the air raid sirens went off and we all rushed to take shelter, I passed the time drawing sounds and vibrations. What I couldn't see but felt. My memory recorded, my hand translated into waves, sensations, impacts. A kind of synaesthetic effect that then found its way into my paintings.

Is painting politics?

It is when it denounces human dramas and prevarications. Oppression and greed. One of the paintings on display, *The Rise of the Blond*, shows a blond figure crossing the canvas with his whole retinue. I would have liked to call it 'The Fall of the Blond'. The reference to the American government is evident, but I didn't want to be didactic about it. The painting engages with political, economic and racial issues. A heterogeneous crowd of beasts march in a celebratory but grotesque parade. The leader displays his unmistakeable yellow forelock and wears a kind of Venetian beak mask on his face, like the ones used during the plague. It is said that artists are able to foresee events. I painted it in 2016, shortly before the election of Donald Trump. It was a genuinely premonitory allegory. So here is another hell.

There's no hope then?
One can always find hope, even in chaos. In one painting, for example, there is the line of a staircase climbing upwards. And lots of light emerging from the background, like in an epiphany.

Like in the *The Scream*, which seems to conceal Beato Angelico's *Incoronation of the Virgin* in the colour?
From Brueghel's landscapes to Goya's *Caprichos*, there are lots of motifs hovering in the background of my works; the eyes and the mind relate them to known images. I didn't think of Beato Angelico in any specific way.
But I love the Italian Renaissance, its iconography and symbols, in addition to the classical equilibrium, the perspective and the depth, which now nurture my scenarios deriving from a mental process. My figures dwell in a place of the mind where the art history of the past encounters our existence.

Hypocrisy of Democracy
Museo
Stefano Bardini

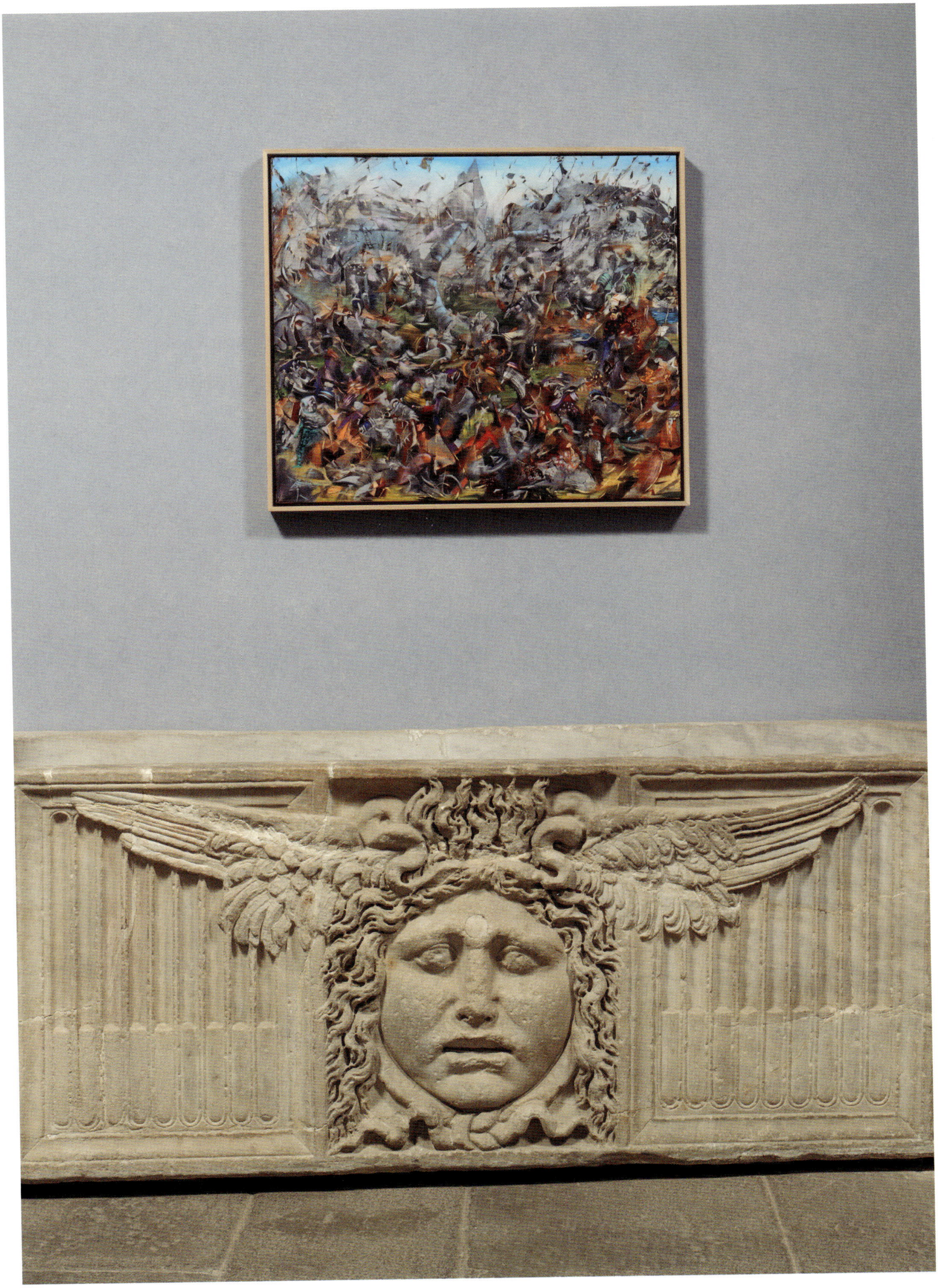

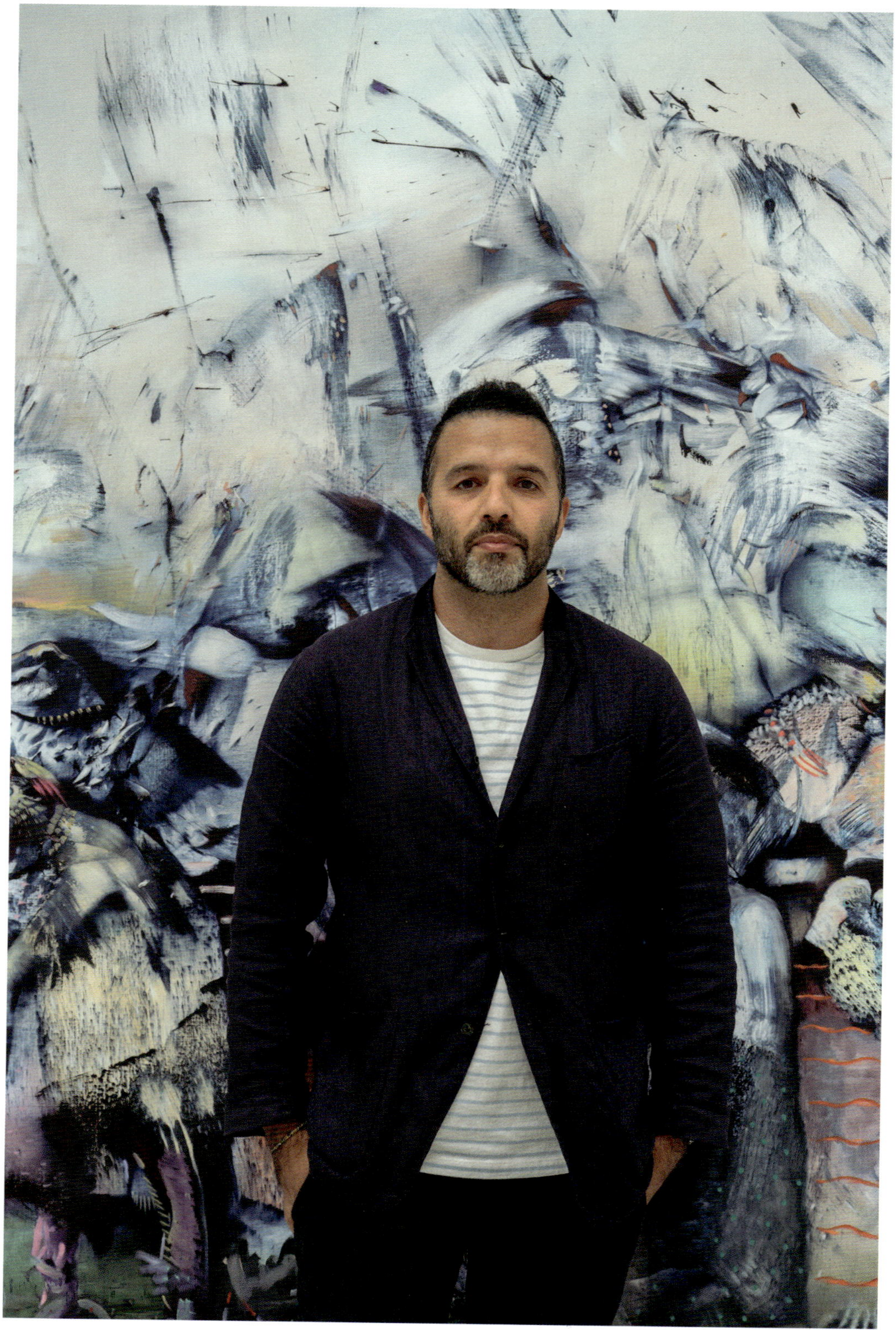

Portrait of Ali Banisadr
Photo by Charles Duprat

Born in Tehran in 1976, Ali Banisadr moved to California with his family when he was a child. While living in San Francisco, he studied psychology and became involved with graffiti art. He has lived and worked in New York since 2000, when he moved to the city to study at the School of Visual Arts and the New York Academy of Art.

Since his first solo exhibition in 2008, his work has been shown at numerous museums, including S.M.A.K. – Stedelijk Museum voor Actuele Kunst, Ghent (2010); Kunstmuseum Den Haag, The Hague (2011); The Met – Metropolitan Museum of Art, New York (2012); Lehmbruck Musem, Duisburg, Germany (2013); Aga Khan Museum, Toronto (2017); The Museum of Fine Arts, Houston (2017).

He was included in *Love Me/Love Me Not: Contemporary Art from Azerbaijan and Its Neighbours* at the 55th Venice Biennale (2013) and in a two-person show with Andrew Sendor at the MOCA – Museum of Contemporary Art, Jacksonville, USA (2019).

Recent solo exhibitions include the Het Noordbrabants Museum, 's-Hertogenbosch, Netherlands (2019); Benaki Museum, Athens (2020); and Wadsworth Atheneum Museum of Art, Hartford, USA (2020).

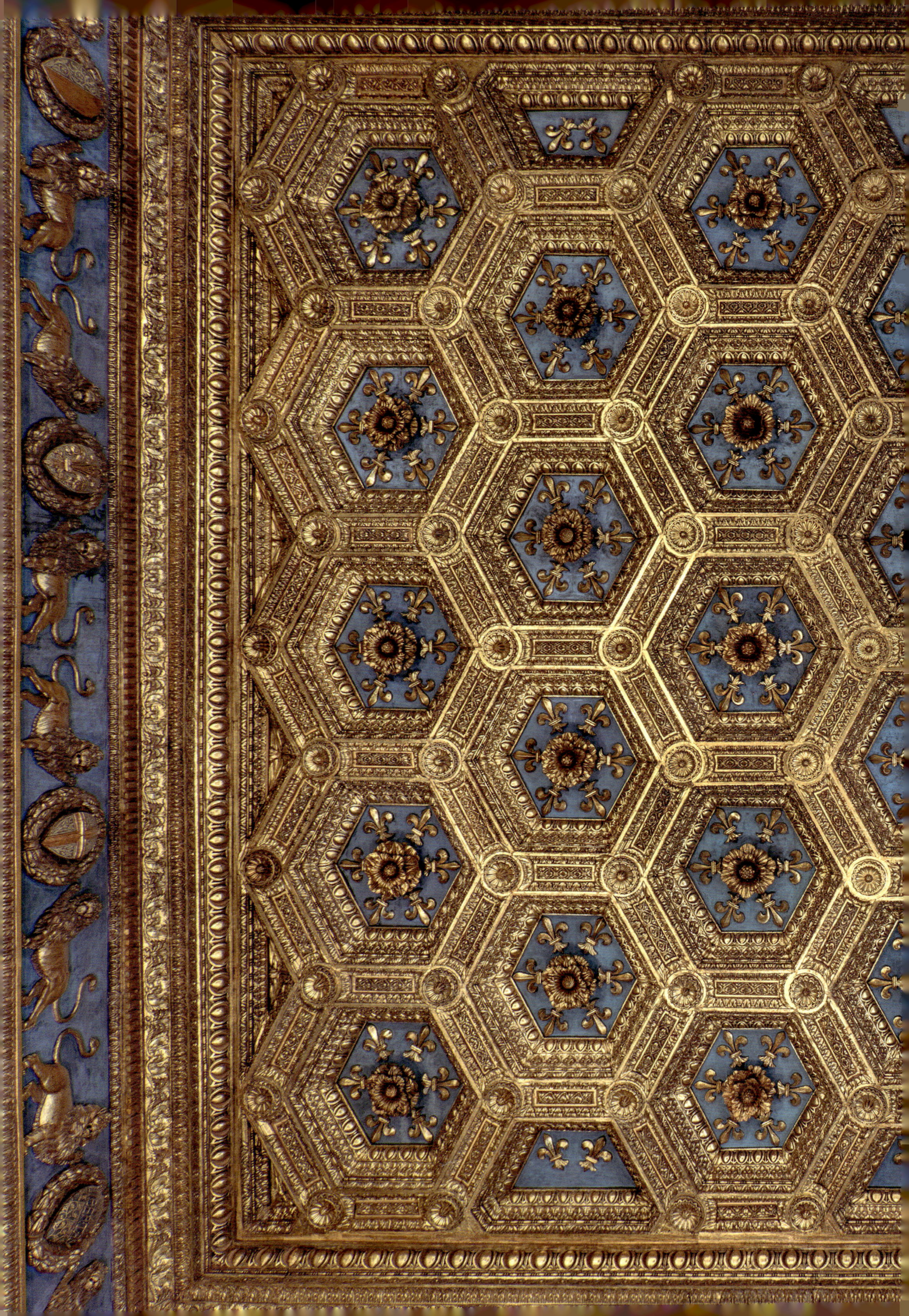

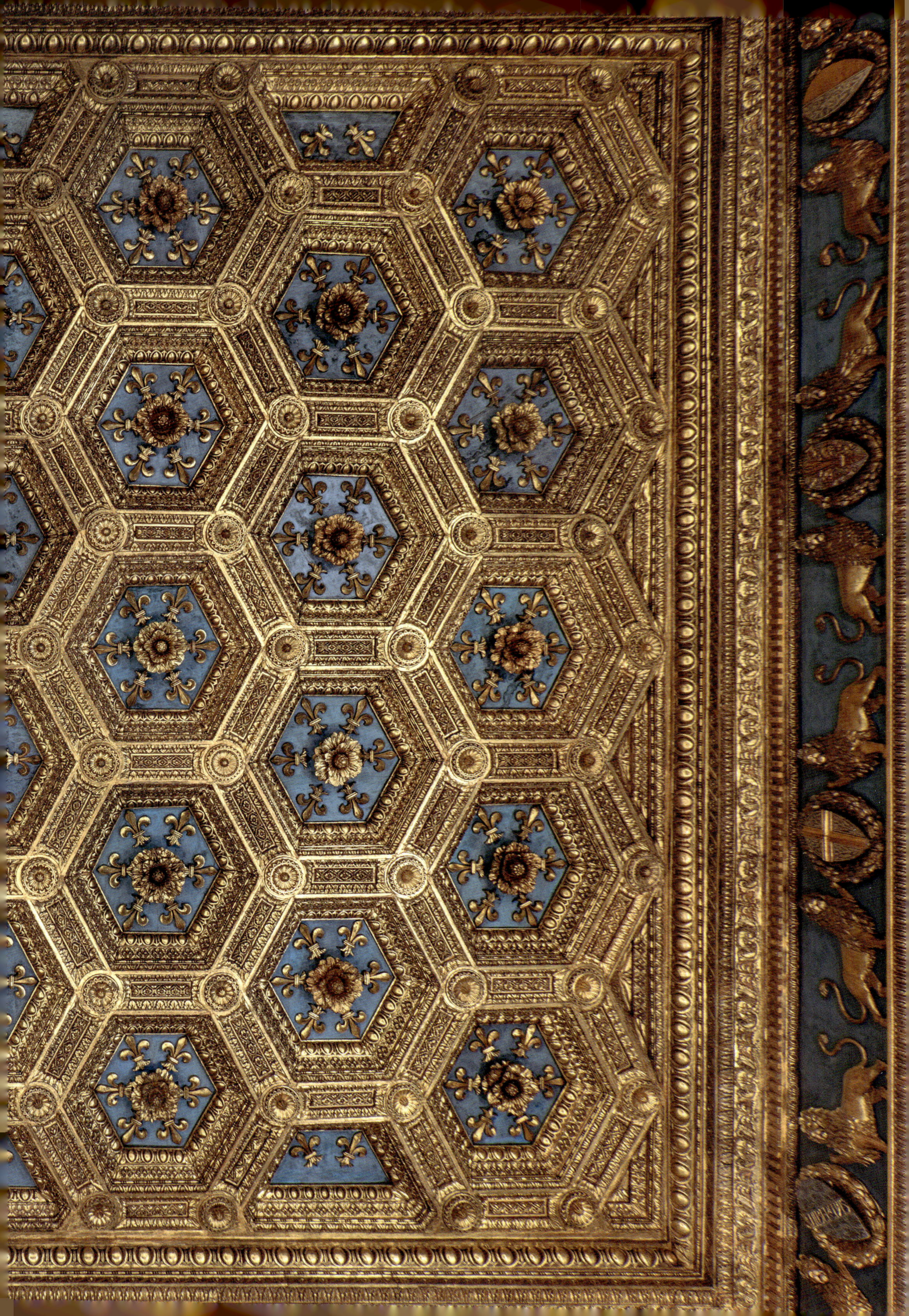

Pages 94-95:
Museo di Palazzo Vecchio,
Ceiling of the Sala dei Gigli

This volume was printed in July 2022
by Lito Terrazzi, Prato, Italy